1986

Writing Essays About Literature

A GUIDE AND STYLE SHEET

KELLEY GRIFFITH, JR.

University of North Carolina at Greensboro

HARCOURT BRACE JOVANOVICH, INC.

New York   San Diego   Chicago   San Francisco   Atlanta
London   Sydney   Toronto

For Gareth and Bronwen

COPYRIGHTS AND ACKNOWLEDGMENTS

The author wishes to acknowledge the following for permission to reprint material used in this book.

HARCOURT BRACE JOVANOVICH for excerpts from *The Oedipus Rex of Sophocles:* An English Version by Dudley Fitts and Robert Fitzgerald. Reprinted by permission of Harcourt Brace Jovanovich, Inc.; copyright 1949 by Harcourt Brace Jovanovich, Inc.; copyright 1977 by Cornelia Fitts and Robert Fitzgerald. And for excerpts from *The Misanthrope* by Molière, reprinted by permission of Harcourt Brace Jovanovich, Inc.; translated and copyright © 1954, 1955 by Richard Wilbur.

HARVARD UNIVERSITY PRESS for the poem "Because I Could Not Stop for Death," by Emily Dickinson. Reprinted by permission of the publishers and the Trustees of Amherst College from *The Poems of Emily Dickinson,* edited by Thomas H. Johnson, Cambridge, MA: The Belknap Press of Harvard University Press, copyright 1951 © 1955, 1979 by the President and Fellows of Harvard College.

HOLT, RINEHART AND WINSTON for ten lines from "The Death of the Hired Man," from *The Poetry of Robert Frost,* edited by Edward Connery Lathem. Copyright 1930, 1939, © 1969 by Holt, Rinehart and Winston. Copyright © 1958 by Robert Frost. Copyright © 1967 by Lesley Frost Ballantine. Reprinted by permission of Holt, Rinehart and Winston, Publishers.

PROFESSOR LEO MARX for permission to reprint the passage from the essay "Mr. Eliot, Mr. Trilling, and *Huckleberry Finn,"* by Leo Marx.

ISBN: 0-15-597860-8

Library of Congress Catalog Card Number: 81-84745

Printed in the United States of America

Preface

I wrote this book in response to a need that constantly emerges in my literature courses. When I assign out-of-class essays, students usually ask a hatbox full of questions: "How do I find something to write about? What should I look for? What do you mean by a critical analysis? What do you consider a good topic? How can I tell if I have written enough? How can I find information about the work? Are we supposed to use footnotes?" The most soulful plea of all is, "I have never written an essay about literature. I'm lost. I have no idea how to begin or what I'm supposed to do. Can you explain what you want?" This plaint comes from a variety of students—even, sometimes, from English majors in upper-level courses. After hearing these questions over and over again, I realized that I wanted to provide my students with a book that would not only offer them the assistance they needed but would cover systematically and thoroughly all aspects of writing essays about literature.

Writing Essays About Literature: A Guide and Style Sheet is my attempt to create such a work. It is, in part, a step-by-step "how-to" book. It takes the student from general to quite specific considerations. The first chapter establishes a rationale for writing essays about literature by making the overriding point of the book—that essays about literature are almost always arguments and, as such, must persuade an audience. The next five chapters confront the most bedeviling problem that student writers face when they write about literature: generating topics. After explaining the most important elements of each genre, as well as the major critical approaches to literature, these chapters offer suggestions and questions to help students work up essay topics on their own. Succeeding chapters deal with rhetorical and mechanical matters that instructors often do not have time to cover in class—supporting a topic, developing a style, achieving logical organization, handling quotations and punctuation correctly, preparing final copies of essays. The chapter on documentation deals with research papers, a kind of essay that many students find vexing, while the chapter on taking tests offers advice about writing in-class essays.

The book concludes with six student essays—two each on a short story, a poem, and a play—all of which illustrate good principles of literary analysis.

The book is not meant to be an all-inclusive treatment of the study of literature; rather, it explains succinctly how to go about the rewarding task of analyzing literature. The work can be used in many ways. Instructors can use it as a textbook in introductory courses or as a supplement in more advanced courses. Students can use it on their own as a guide to writing essays about literature, as an introduction to the study of literature, and as a reference manual.

I owe many people gratitude for their help. I am indebted to the writers whose works I have consulted. I thank my colleagues Walter Beale and William Tucker for reading and criticizing this work in its initial stages. During the later stages of revision, I incorporated the valuable comments of other readers: Laurence Perrine; Frank Garratt, Tacoma Community College; George Gleason, Southwest Missouri State University; John Hanes, Duquesne University; Jacqueline Hartwich, Bellevue Community College; and Irving Howe, Hunter College and the Graduate Center of the City University of New York. And I am deeply grateful to my family for the encouragement they always give me.

KELLEY GRIFFITH, JR.

Contents

6 *How to Generate Topics by Evaluating the Quality of Literature* 80

7 *How to Create Good Essay Content* 89

1

The essay about literature

L IKE ALL ART, literature gives pleasure. It has a certain magic that transports us from the "real" world to a seemingly more remote and enjoyable place. You can experience this quality without analyzing it. But literature also poses intellectual challenges that do demand analysis. For most readers, grappling with these challenges enhances the pleasure of literature. By studying literature, you "see" more of it to appreciate. And you learn that, far from being remote from life, good literature pleases you by reflecting and giving order to life.

ESSAYS ABOUT LITERATURE ARE ARGUMENTS

Essays about literature are written works that take up the intellectual challenges posed by literature. They raise and try to answer fascinating and puzzling questions: How does the work reflect its time? How does it reflect the author's life and thought? What does it mean? How does it work? Is it good art? Has it had an impact on society? What human problems does it portray? But you will write better essays if you recognize another quality of essays about literature: they are almost always arguments.

This quality emerges from the relationship between the work and its reader. Good literature is complex. It communicates on

1

many levels of meaning and by many methods. A single work may exist as a system of sounds, of symbols, of ideas, of images, of analogies, of actions, of psychological portrayals, of actions, of moods—all of which are separate entities, yet all of which interrelate. As a result, perceptions of a work vary from age to age, reader to reader, even reading to reading. This variability of perception occurs because no single reading, no matter how careful, can take in all the elements of a work or synthesize them into all their structural relationships.

Consequently, no single view of a work, whether your own or someone else's, can be the all-encompassing or final view. Cultures change, people change, and as a result perception changes. It is a common experience for children to enjoy works—*Huckleberry Finn, Gulliver's Travels,* "Rip Van Winkle"—and as adults to enjoy them again, but for very different reasons and with entirely new understandings of them. This does not mean that all interpretations of a work are equally valid. Interpretations of literature are subject to the same rules of human thought—accurate observation, sound logic, systematic procedure, thoroughness of treatment—as any other type of analysis. But no *single* interpretation can encompass the whole work.

Because literature is complex and *because* it can be perceived variously, essays about literature are usually arguments. That is, the writer offers an opinion (a thesis) and tries to persuade his or her readers to accept it.

A LITERARY CONTROVERSY

The people who make a profession of writing essays about literature are called "literary critics," and the product of their writing is "literary criticism." Literary criticism is not "criticism" in the sense that it searches out and exposes the bad qualities of something. Rather, literary criticism analyzes literature. Its purpose is to explain works of literature to interested readers. When you write essays about literature, you are writing literary criticism.

The essays described and excerpted below were written by professional literary critics, and they illustrate the argumentative nature of essays about literature. These essays deal with what has become a famous literary controversy—the controversy over the ending of Mark Twain's *The Adventures of Huckleberry Finn*. *Huckleberry Finn* is a great novel because of its realistic depiction of Mississippi Valley culture, its complex character development, its rich themes, its humor, and its poetic language. Four-fifths of the way through the novel, however, Twain changes the tone and implication of the narrative from subtle comedy to ridiculous farce. Most readers find this part of the novel disappointing.

A full-blown literary controversy began when two well-known critics defended the ending. Lionel Trilling, in an introduction to the novel, published in 1948 (New York: Rinehart Editions, 1948, pp. xv–xvi), had this to say about the ending:

> In form and style *Huckleberry Finn* is an almost perfect work. Only one mistake has ever been charged against it, that it concludes with Tom Sawyer's elaborate, too elaborate, game of Jim's escape. Certainly this episode is too long—in the original draft it was much longer—and certainly it is a falling-off, as almost anything would have to be, from the incidents of the river. Yet it has a certain formal aptness—like, say, that of the Turkish initiation which brings Molière's *Le Bourgeois Gentilhomme* to its close. It is a rather mechanical development of an idea, and yet some device is needed to permit Huck to return to his anonymity, to give up the role of hero, to fall into the background which he prefers, for he is modest in all things and could not well endure the attention and glamour which attend a hero at a book's end. For this purpose nothing could serve better than the mind of Tom Sawyer with its literary furnishings, its conscious romantic desire for experience and the hero's part, and its ingenious schematization of life to acheive that aim.

T. S. Eliot, in an introduction to another edition of the novel (London: Cresset Press, 1950, pp. xv–xvi), essentially agreed with Trilling:

> Readers sometimes deplore the fact that the story descends to the level of *Tom Sawyer* from the moment that Tom himself re-appears. Such readers protest that the escapades invented by Tom, in the attempted "rescue" of Jim, are only a

tedious development of themes with which we are already too familiar—even while admitting that the escapades themselves are very amusing, and some of the incidental observations memorable. But it is right that the mood of the end of the book should bring us back to that of the beginning. Or, if this was not the right ending for the book, what ending would have been right? . . . For Huckleberry Finn, neither a tragic nor a happy ending would be suitable. No worldly success or social satisfaction, no domestic consummation would be worthy of him; a tragic end also would reduce him to the level of those whom we pity. Huck Finn must come from nowhere and be bound for nowhere. . . . Hence, he can only disappear; and his disappearance can only be accomplished by bringing forward another performer to obscure the disappearance in a cloud of whimsicalities.

The result was an outpouring of essays responding to Trilling's and Eliot's opinions. One cogent response is Leo Marx's "Mr. Eliot, Mr. Trilling, and *Huckleberry Finn*," which originally appeared in *The American Scholar* in 1953. The first few paragraphs of the essay appear below and represent the main thrust of Marx's argument.

MR. ELIOT, MR. TRILLING, AND *HUCKLEBERRY FINN*

LEO MARX

The *Adventures of Huckleberry Finn* has not always occupied its present high place in the canon of American literature. When it was first published in 1885, the book disturbed and offended many reviewers, particularly spokesmen for the genteel tradition. In fact, a fairly accurate inventory of the narrow standards of such critics might be made simply by listing epithets they applied to Clemens' novel. They called it vulgar, rough, inelegant, irreverent, coarse, semi-obscene, trashy and vicious. So much for them. Today (we like to think) we know the true worth of the book. Everyone now agrees that *Huckleberry Finn* is a masterpiece: it is probably the one book in our literature about which highbrows and lowbrows can agree. Our most serious critics praise it. Nevertheless, a close look at what two of the best among them have recently written will likewise reveal, I believe, serious weaknesses in current criticism. Today the problem of evaluating the book is as much obscured by unqualified praise as it once was by parochial hostility.

I have in mind essays by Lionel Trilling and T. S. Eliot. Both praise the book, but in praising it both feel obligated to say something in justification of what so many readers have felt to be its great flaw: the disappointing "ending," the episode which begins when Huck arrives at the Phelps place and Tom Sawyer reappears. There are good reasons why Mr. Trilling and Mr. Eliot should feel the need to face this issue. From the point of view of scope alone, more is involved than the mere "ending"; the episode comprises almost one-fifth of the text. The problem, in any case, is unavoidable. I have discussed *Huckleberry Finn* in courses with hundreds of college students, and I have found only a handful who did not confess their dissatisfaction with the extravagant mock rescue of Nigger Jim and the denouement itself. The same question always comes up: "What went wrong with Twain's novel?" Even Bernard De Voto, whose wholehearted commitment to Clemens' genius is well known, has said of the ending that "in the whole reach of the English novel there is no more abrupt or more chilling descent."* Mr. Trilling and Mr. Eliot do not agree. They both attempt, and on similar grounds, to explain and defend the conclusion.

Of the two, Mr. Trilling makes the more moderate claim for Clemens' novel. He does admit that there is a "falling off" at the end; nevertheless he supports the episode as having "a certain formal aptness." Mr. Eliot's approval is without serious qualification. He allows no objections, asserts that "it is right that the mood of the end of the book should bring us back to the beginning." I mean later to discuss their views in some detail, but here it is only necessary to note that both critics see the problem as one of form. And so it is. Like many questions of form in literature, however, this one is not finally separable from a question of "content," of value, or, if you will, of, moral insight. To bring *Huckleberry Finn* to a satisfactory close, Clemens had to do more than find a neat device for ending a story. His problem, though it may never have occurred to him, was to invent an action capable of placing in focus the meaning of the journey down the Mississippi.

I believe that the ending of *Huckleberry Finn* makes so many readers uneasy because they rightly sense that it jeopardizes the significance of the entire novel. To take seriously what happens at the Phelps farm is to take lightly the entire downstream journey. What is the meaning of the

Mark Twain at Work (Cambridge, 1942), p. 92.

journey? With this question all discussion of *Huckleberry Finn* must begin. It is true that the voyage down the river has many aspects of a boy's idyl. We owe much of its hold upon our imagination to the enchanting image of the raft's unhurried drift with the current. The leisure, the absence of constraint, the beauty of the river—all these things delight us. "It's lovely to live on a raft." And the multitudinous life of the great valley we see through Huck's eyes has a fascination of its own. Then, of course, there is humor—laughter so spontaneous, so free of bitterness present almost everywhere in American humor that readers often forget how grim a spectacle of human existence Huck contemplates. Humor in this novel flows from a bright joy of life as remote from our world as living on a raft.

Yet along with the idyllic and the epical and the funny in *Huckleberry Finn,* there is a coil of meaning which does for the disparate elements of the novel what a spring does for a watch. The meaning is not in the least obscure. It is made explicit again and again. The very words with which Clemens launches Huck and Jim upon their voyage indicate that theirs is not a boy's lark but a quest for freedom. From the electrifying moment when Huck comes back to Jackson's Island and rouses Jim with the news that a search party is on the way, we are meant to believe that Huck is enlisted in the cause of freedom. "Git up and hump yourself, Jim!" he cries. "There ain't a minute to lose. They're after us!" What particularly counts here is the *us*. No one is after Huck; no one but Jim knows he is alive. In that small word Clemens compresses the exhilarating power of Huck's instinctive humanity. His unpremeditated identification with Jim's flight from slavery is an unforgettable moment in American experience, and it may be said at once that any culmination of the journey which detracts from the urgency and dignity with which it begins will necessarily be unsatisfactory. Huck realizes this himself, and says so when, much later, he comes back to the raft after discovering that the Duke and the King have sold Jim:

> "After all this long journey . . . here it was all come to nothing, everything all busted up and ruined, because they could have the heart to serve Jim such a trick as that, and make him a slave again all his life, and amongst strangers, too, for forty dirty dollars."

Huck knows that the journey will have been a failure unless it takes Jim to freedom. It is true that we do discover, in the end, that Jim is free, but we also find out that the journey was not the means by which he finally reached freedom.

The most obvious thing wrong with the end, then, is the flimsy contrivance by which Clemens frees Jim. In the end we not only discover that Jim has been a free man for two months, but that his freedom has been granted by old Miss Watson. If this were only a mechanical device for terminating the action, it might not call for much comment. But it is more than that: it is a significant clue to the import of the last ten chapters. Remember who Miss Watson is. She is the Widow's sister whom Huck introduces in the first pages of the novel. It is she who keeps "pecking" at Huck, who tries to teach him to spell and to pray and to keep his feet off the furniture. She is an ardent proselytizer for piety and good manners, and her greed provides the occasion for the journey in the first place. She is Jim's owner, and he decides to flee only when he realizes that she is about to break her word (she cannot resist a slave trader's offer of eight hundred dollars) and sell him down the river away from his family.

Miss Watson, in short, is the Enemy. If we except a predilection for physical violence, she exhibits all the outstanding traits of the valley society. She pronounces the polite lies of civilization that suffocate Huck's spirit. The freedom which Jim seeks, and which Huck and Jim temporarily enjoy aboard the raft, is accordingly freedom *from* everything for which Miss Watson stands. Indeed, the very intensity of the novel derives from the discordance between the aspirations of the fugitives and the respectable code for which she is a spokesman. Therefore, her regeneration, of which the deathbed freeing of Jim is the unconvincing sign, hints a resolution of the novel's essential conflict. Perhaps because this device most transparently reveals that shift in point of view which he could not avoid, and which is less easily discerned elsewhere in the concluding chapters, Clemens plays it down. He makes little attempt to account for Miss Watson's change of heart, a change particularly surprising in view of Jim's brazen escape. Had Clemens given this episode dramatic emphasis appropriate to its function, Miss Watson's bestowal of freedom upon Jim would have proclaimed what the rest of the ending actually accomplishes—a vindication of persons and attitudes Huck and Jim had symbolically repudiated when they set forth downstream.

It may be said, and with some justice, that a reading of the ending as a virtual reversal of meanings implicit in the rest of the novel misses the point—that I have taken the final episode too seriously. I agree that Clemens certainly did not intend us to read it so solemnly. The ending, one might contend, is simply a burlesque upon Tom's taste for literary romance. Surely the tone of the episode is familiar to readers of Mark Twain. The preposterous monkey business attendant upon Jim's "rescue," the careless improvisation, the nonchalant disregard for common-sense plausibility—all these things should not surprise readers of Twain or any low comedy in the tradition of "Western humor." However, the trouble is, first, that the ending hardly comes off as burlesque: it is *too* fanciful, *too* extravagant; and it is tedious. For example, to provide a "gaudy" atmosphere for the escape, Huck and Tom catch a couple of dozen snakes. Then the snakes escape.

> "No, there warn't no real scarcity of snakes about the house for a considerable spell. You'd see them dripping from the rafters and places every now and then; and they generly landed in your plate, or down the back of your neck. . . ."

Even if this were *good* burlesque, which it is not, what is it doing here? It is out of keeping; the slapstick tone jars with the underlying seriousness of the voyage.

Huckleberry Finn is a masterpiece because it brings Western humor to perfection and yet transcends the narrow limits of its conventions. But the ending does not. During the final extravaganza we are forced to put aside many of the mature emotions evoked earlier by the vivid rendering of Jim's fear of capture, the tenderness of Huck's and Jim's regard for each other, and Huck's excruciating moments of wavering between honesty and respectability. None of these emotions are called forth by the anticlimactic final sequence. I do not mean to suggest that the inclusion of low comedy per se is a flaw in *Huckleberry Finn.* One does not object to the shenanigans of the rogues; there is ample precedent for the place of extravagant humor even in works of high seriousness. But here the case differs from most which come to mind: the major characters themselves are forced to play low comedy roles. Moreover, the most serious motive in the novel, Jim's yearning for freedom, is made the object of nonsense. The conclusion, in short, is farce, but the rest of the novel is not.

The rest of Marx's essay is a thorough response to each point made by Trilling and Eliot. After Marx published his essay, other critics wrote essays responding to his points. You, of course, must decide for yourself which side of the controversy is more compelling. The point to remember is that these essays—like most essays about literature—are arguments. Each writer offers a thesis and accepts the obligation to defend that thesis with evidence and logic.

2

How to analyze literature

THE FIRST STEP in writing a good essay about literature is to read the work well. You read well when you analyze what you have read. This skill is not the same as reading for "comprehension," which means recording mentally the information given in a work. Reading for comprehension is an essential preliminary skill for reading literature well. But to read analytically is to develop *ideas about* the information contained in a work. Analyzing something means breaking it down into its components and discovering the relationship among them, the relationship that gives unity and coherence to the whole. In order to do this for works of literature, you need to know what literature is, what components you can typically expect in the works you read and how they typically relate. This chapter offers a "definition," an overview of literature that should help you begin the process of analysis. The two chapters immediately following this one discuss the elements of literature in greater detail. All three chapters should help you to analyze works of literature thoroughly and carefully and therefore should help you to write essays about them.

There are enough mysterious elements in "literature" to make a complete definition impossible. Critics who have tried to define it, however, agree on a few common elements.

1. LITERATURE IS LANGUAGE

The medium of literature is language, both oral and written. But not everything that is written or spoken is literature. Creators of literature use language in a special way, a way different from that of scientists or people using everyday speech. Scientists use language for its *denotative* value, its ability to provide symbols (words) that mean one thing precisely. For scientists, the thing that the symbol represents—the referent—is more important than the symbol itself. Any symbol will do, as long as it represents the referent clearly and exactly. Since emotions render meanings imprecise, scientists try to use symbols that eliminate the emotional, the irrational, the subjective.

Writers of literature, in contrast, use language *connotatively*. They may at times—as in realistic novels—emphasize denotation, but usually they employ the connotative meanings of language. Connotation is the meaning that attaches to words in addition to their explicit referents. A good example of the difference between denotation and connotation is the word "mother," whose denotation is simply "female parent" but whose connotations include nurturance, warmth, unqualified love, tenderness, devotion, protection, mercy, intercession, home, childhood, the happier past. The connotative meanings of words are subjective, multiple, and sometimes arbitrary. Even scientific language becomes connotative once it enters everyday speech. For the formula $E = mc^2$, one no longer thinks just of "Energy equals mass times the speed of light squared" but of mushroom clouds, ruined cities, and a long-haired genius padding about his house in bedroom slippers.

Writers of literature use language, in short, for its expressive and emotional qualities. But they also use it for itself. They are fascinated by its sounds, its rhythms, even its appearance on the page. Sometimes they become so interested in these qualities that they subordinate meaning to them. People who use language in everyday speech and writing also display a sensitivity to its sounds and subjective qualities, but writers of literature exploit these qualities more fully, more consciously, and more systematically.

As you read, then, you should pay attention to the way the author uses language. You should note the choice of words *(diction)*, the sentence structure *(syntax)*, the sound qualities of the language, the connotations and double meanings of key words, the various dialects used in the characters' dialogue. Part of this attention to language should help you simply to understand the work. You should, for example, always look up words that are unfamiliar to you but that seem crucial to understanding a passage, especially in poetry.

2. LITERATURE IS AESTHETIC

Another quality of literature is that it gives a unique pleasure. This aesthetic quality cannot be defined and described. It just *is*. Like other aesthetic pleasures—music, patterns of color, sunsets, dance—literature is an end in itself.

All the elements of literature contribute to the pleasure it gives, but probably the most important is *form,* the order that the writer imposes on the materials—on language, characters, events, details—all of which he or she draws from the usually disorderly realm of real life. Take, for example, events. In real life, events are not necessarily related by cause and effect. Or if some events are related, many are not. Events don't necessarily lead to a conclusion. This murderer may not be caught, the cruel parent may go on being cruel, the economic crisis may not be resolved, the poor but honest youth may not be rewarded. There are so many events in a person's life that it is hard to remember or even be aware of them all. We don't always know which events are important, which trivial. But literature can give order to events in the form of a *plot*. Unimportant events will be excluded, cause-and-effect relationships established, conflicts introduced and resolved. Events will be arranged in logical order so that they form a sequence with a beginning, middle, and end. They may even have suspense, so that we fearfully or gleefully anticipate what will happen next. Plot, of course, is only one of a multitude of ways in which the artist gives order to the material. He or she may also arrange language into orderly patterns, reduce characters to recognizable types, offer ideas that guide the reader toward a certain interpretation of the material, describe settings in a selective, logical way. In a good work of literature, all of the elements combine to create an *overall* order, an *overall* coherence.

As you read, then, look for anything that gives pattern or structure to the work. This can be forms imposed upon the language—like the sonnet or ballad form for poetry. It can be the handling of time—how many hours, days, months, years the story covers. It can be act and scene divisions of plays, chapter divisions of novels, stanza and line divisions of poetry. It can be repetitions of phrases, words, images, metaphors. It can be *anything* that the use of language will allow, whether traditional and easily recognizable or innovative and difficult at first to see.

3. LITERATURE IS FICTIONAL

We commonly use the term "fiction" to describe prose works that tell a story (short stories and novels). In fact, however, all works of literature are "fictional" in the sense that the reader sets them apart from the facts of real life.

A work can be fictional in two ways. First, the writer makes up some of the materials. Some of the characters, events, dialogue, and settings exist only in the writer's imagination. He or she may draw upon real-life observations and experiences to create them; but when these appear in the finished work, they have been so altered that no one-to-one correlation can be said to exist between them and anything that actually exists or existed. The writer may, furthermore, ignore laws that govern the real world. An obvious example is fantasy fiction, wherein human beings fly, perform magic, confront dragons, remain young, travel through time, discover utopian kingdoms, metamorphose, live happily ever after, or where animals or other "creatures" take on human traits, like speech and intelligence. But even historical fiction, which relies on actual events for some of its material, is fictional. It includes characters, dialogue, events, and settings that do not exist in history.

Second, in addition to a lack of factuality, the fictionality of literature lies in the artistic control the writer exercises over the work. This artistic control has the effect of stylizing the materials of the work and thus setting the work apart from the context of the real. This effect occurs even when the material of the work *does* accurately mirror the facts of real life or when it states ideas that can be verified in actual experience. Compare, for example, accounts of the same event written by a newspaper reporter and by a poet. Both writers may describe the event accurately, but the reporter makes his or her account correspond as exactly as possible to the event, so that the reader will experience the details of the event, not the report of it. The poet, in contrast, makes his or her *poem* the object of experience. Through the use of language, the selection of details, the interpretation—stated or implied—of the event, the inclusion of devices like metaphor, irony, and imagery, the poet makes the work an artifact, an object of enjoyment and contemplation in itself. The reader instinctively if not consciously recognizes it as different from the event itself. In this way, the work becomes "fictional." Because of this element of fictionality you can experience and even enjoy works whose subject matter would in real life be so depressing or horrifying as to be unendurable.

You can detect the fictional quality of a work most obviously by watching for those elements that depart from the norms of reality. Less obvious but equally important are those elements that make the work an object of scrutiny in and for itself, such as its use of language and its ordering of material. One of the most important effects of the fictionality of literature is the distance it creates between you and the material presented. This distance is both physical and psychological. You know, as you read, that you are not actually involved in the work's events. They are physically, safely removed from you. Thus you can give freer rein to your emotional reactions than you can for real events. It would be difficult to control your emotions were you to to meet a real vampire, or werewolf, or homicidal maniac. But you can indulge in, enjoy, and yet control your feelings of fright by confronting yourself with fictional ones. Some authors, however, try to reduce as much as they can the psychological distance between their fictional events and you. They want to draw you into the events so fully that, at least for the moment, you imagine you are involved in real events. Other authors, in contrast, like Nicolai Gogol, Henry Fielding, Washington Irving, and W. M. Thackeray, constantly remind you that their events are fictional. One thing you might do when you read, then, is try to gauge the distance between you and the material of the work. Does the author minimize this distance or emphasize it? How and why?

4. LITERATURE IS TRUE

Even though, as we have just seen, works of literature are "fictional," they have the capacity for being "true." This paradox creates one of the most important and pleasurable tensions in literature—the fictionality of literature as against its truthfulness in conveying the reality of human experience. Literature can be faithful to the facts of reality, as in descriptive prose and poetry. But it can be true in two other, more important ways. First, it interprets the real world, even when it distorts, ignores, or alters facts. Simple examples of the interpretive quality of literature are fables and fairy tales, whose characters and events may be fantastic but whose lessons are true to our own experience. Aesop's fox in the "sour grapes" story is like no fox in real life; he can reason and use language. But he behaves like a real person in similar circumstances, and the lesson we learn from his behavior is a shrewd commentary on human nature.

Unlike fables, however, most literature does not present its interpretations of life in the form of a moral tacked on at the end. Rather, the total form of a work represents its interpretation. A work of literature creates an imaginary "world," and this world embodies a theory about how the real world works. That is, it embodies a "world view." The author may or may not be directly aware of this theory, but his or her view of the real world inevitably influences his or her construction of the imaginary one. In turn, we can infer the author's world view from the details of his or her created world. Thus, the world of George Orwell's *1984* is filled with crumbling buildings, frightened people, children who spitefully turn their parents over to the police, procedures whereby truth is systematically altered, masses of people trapped by their ignorance and selfishness, officials who justify any deed to achieve power. It is a world without love, compassion, justice, joy, tradition, altruism, idealism, or hope. The facts of this world are patently imaginary—Orwell himself placed them in the future—but they communicate Orwell's extremely pessimistic view of human nature and human institutions. Orwell is showing that, given what he has observed of today's society, he believes that the terrible society he describes in *1984* could become a reality.

What specific devices do authors use to embody their world views in their works? Two important ones are the representation of

typical characters and of probable actions. Because works of literature often clothe their worlds in manifold detail, they create the
illusion of being real and thus unique. But the characters and events
of literature cannot be unique if they are to be meaningful. We
often encounter freakish, inexplicable events and people in real life,
and they disturb us because we cannot place them within an orderly
context. But we expect literature to give order to the chaos of real
life, and it does so partly by exposing patterns of meaning in life.
In order to do this, literature must conform to generally recognizable patterns of behavior and probability. J. R. R. Tolkien, for example, offers an array of fantasy creatures and kingdoms in *The
Hobbit* and its sequel, *The Lord of the Rings*. Yet his characters, whatever they may look like, represent types of human behavior,
and the events in which they participate represent human activities
that we recognize as characteristic of individuals, clans, organiza-
tions, and nations. The protagonists, Bilbo and Frodo Baggins, ty-
pify those gentle, kindly people who would much prefer to live in
domestic obscurity but who are called on to play heroic roles in a
cataclysmic drama. And the way they behave is probable, because
it fits the type of person they are. They don't suddenly become
supermen with supernatural powers. Like the average person, they
are vulnerable to superior strength and to their own fears and
temptations. But they succeed because they exhibit the strengths of
the average person—perseverance, shrewdness, unselfishness, courage, and honesty.

Of course, world views expressed in works of literature are
subjective. The authors are expressing *their* views of what the real
world is like. Orwell's view is very different from Tolkien's. Orwell
shows an average man rebelling against social corruption and fail-
ing miserably to do anything about it. He is weak, ineffective, and
controlled by forces outside himself. In Orwell's world, good loses
out because people are too stupid or too greedy or too weak to
overcome evil. Like Orwell, Tolkien also shows the average man as
weak, but in his world view, the average person is innately good
and potentially strong; such individuals can band together with
others like themselves and overthrow evil. Orwell is pessimistic
about human nature and the future of humanity; Tolkien is optimistic.

In addition to offering a world view, literature can be true by
presenting the *experience* of reality. The experience may be new or
old, unique or shared by many people. Whatever it is, the author

uses his or her imagination to put us in the midst of it, to make us feel it. The result is that we understand it better.

An example is Jessamyn West's novel *The Massacre at Fall Creek* (1977). In the afterword she says she had long been intrigued by a historical event that occurred in Indiana in 1824. A white judge and jury convicted four white men for killing Indians, and the men were hanged. As far as West could discover, this event marked the first time in United States history that white men convicted other white men for killing Indians. But she had been able to find little historical information on this episode. She wondered, What must it have been like to be condemned to death for something that had up to then been approved, or at least tolerated? How must the people, Indians and whites alike, have felt about the event? West's novel is an answer to these questions. We cannot *know* what these people experienced, but through an act of the imagination, West shows us what they probably experienced because she can assess what most people would go through under those circumstances. Furthermore, she causes us to *feel* what they experienced. We live through the killings themselves, with all their gruesome details. We share with the whites the fear of Indian reprisal. We see the callousness of hardened Indian killers. We experience the dawning realization of some whites that Indians are human beings and have rights. We suffer the alienation felt by those who take unpopular moral stands. We partake of the circuslike atmosphere of the crowd come to see the hangings. We puzzle over the ambiguity of the ethical problem confronting the judge. We stand on the scaffold with the condemned.

An idea that underlies Jessamyn West's world view is that it is wrong to kill Indians. Or, to put it more generally, she shows that all human life is precious and therefore should not be wantonly destroyed. Like the ideas in most works of literature, this idea is not new or profound. Compare it, for example, with Orwell's in *1984* (totalitarianism is dehumanizing) and Tolkien's in *The Lord of the Rings* (eternal vigilance is the price of freedom). But the abstract ideas that underlie works of literature almost *have* to be commonplace in order to be recognizable and thus universal. The profundity of literature lies in its imaginative reconstruction of the experience of commonplace ideas. We don't have to read *Anna Karenina* to learn that circumstances and moral blindness can drive a person to despair. We read it because Tolstoy, through Anna, makes us *feel what it is like* to have everything we care about taken from us little by little because of flaws in our character or because of blind chance.

There are a number of things you can do to analyze the "truths" within a work.

1. Look for basic themes. Sometimes the author will state them or have a character state them. Usually, however, authors present themes indirectly. Underline or mark events, dialogue, and details of setting that seem to develop a theme.

2. Look for and underline what is typical of characters. Note those things each major character does and says that identify him or her as typical. See if you can tell how the author may be using the typical traits of a character to develop ideas.

3. Analyze the nature of the "world" the author presents. Useful questions to keep in mind are, Is the setting hostile or friendly, ugly or beautiful? Are the characters mean-spirited or friendly, driven by forces beyond their control or operating by free will? Does fate seem to be blind or purposeful (is good rewarded and evil punished)?

4. Note the implications of titles and epigraphs. (An epigraph is a pertinent quotation put at the beginning of a work or a chapter.) *The Grapes of Wrath* (taken from a line in "The Battle Hymn of the Republic"), *All the King's Men* (from the nursery rhyme "Humpty Dumpty"), *Pride and Prejudice, Great Expectations, Measure for Measure* are examples of titles that represent the authors' judgment of what their works are about.

5. Sometimes an author will comment about the work outside the work—in speeches, interviews, and lectures. These may be worth seeking out, especially if the work is puzzling. Flannery O'Connor's comments about "A Good Man Is Hard to Find" are extremely revealing about the story's possible meaning.

6. Mark and reread those sections to which the instructor calls your attention in class.

5. LITERATURE IS EXPRESSIVE

Literature is an expression of the individuals who write it. Their personalities, emotions, and beliefs are bound up in their works. Some authors may try to reduce their presence as much as possible, so that the work seems to be merely that of a faceless observer who transcribes or mirrors reality. Shakespeare's plays and Daniel Defoe's novels have this quality. Other authors make themselves and their feelings the obvious subject matter of their work. William Wordsworth, who wrote that poetry "is the spontaneous overflow of powerful feelings," is one example. Lord Byron and Thomas Wolfe are others. But whatever authors decide about the relationship between themselves and their subject matter, they inevitably stamp it with those qualities that belong uniquely to them. And when we read their works, we feel the force of their presence.

One result of the expressive aspect of literature is that we may be drawn to a work because we are drawn to the author. We are charmed or impressed by the author's presence in the work. And we may read other works by that writer because we want to experience more of him or her. We may read Charlotte Brontë to experience Charlotte Brontë, Ernest Hemingway to experience Ernest Hemingway. Another result—sometimes intended by the author—is that through the work, we experience events and emotional reactions that may be outside our own experience. The work thus broadens the range of our experience.

The expressive element in works of literature is often elusive. It may be solely a matter of language, whereby the author maintains a consistent style from work to work. Or it may be a philosophical outlook that carries over from work to work. Or it may be an autobiographical treatment of events in the author's life. If the expressive aspect of literature interests you, your best bet is to read more than one work by an author and to read about the author. See if you can identify common elements among the works. Another approach is to see if you can identify the author's "voice" in the work. Where and how does the writer make his or her presence felt and his or her ideas known?

6. LITERATURE IS AFFECTIVE

Often related to the expressive aspect of literature is its affective aspect—that is, its ability to create an emotional response in the reader. The aesthetic experience that we discussed earlier is itself emotional, but the other elements of literature create emotional reactions as well. As with the expressive aspect, the degree to which literature is affective varies from author to author. Some writers try to make their works as unemotional and intellectual as possible. Alexander Pope's poetry, for example, appeals to our reasoning ability and to our interest in witty word play. Henry James's novels present moral problems that take on the quality of complicated puzzles. In contrast, other works are awash in sentiment; they want us to feel deeply and sometimes to do something about the situations that evoke feelings in us, as in the case of reform fiction like Charles Dickens' *Oliver Twist* and Harriet Beecher Stowe's *Uncle Tom's Cabin*. Some literary forms—tragedy, comedy, melodrama, the lament, the elegy—strive to elicit fairly specific emotional reactions from us.

The expressive and affective aspects of literature often work together. The author makes the reader feel what he or she has felt. In *Native Son,* Richard Wright puts us in the shoes of a young black man living in an urban ghetto. He intends for us to be shocked by the violent crimes Bigger Thomas commits. But then he wants us to feel what it is like to be a victim of racism and, by feeling it, to see this victimization as a cause of Bigger's crimes. Wright is black, and his point is that the hatred Bigger Thomas feels is typical of black people in the United States, even though most have not committed violent crimes as Bigger has. Wright makes us aware of his feelings by causing us, through his novel, to feel what he has felt.

You can get at the affective elements in works of literature in several ways. Most obvious is to ask yourself what emotions the work raised in you: What "effect" did it have on you? Another is to ask others what effect it had on them: Was it the same as the effect on you? Once you identify the effect, you can ask why the author creates it: What is he or she trying to achieve?

3

How to generate topics about fiction

HOW DO YOU come up with essay topics? What makes a topic "good"? The answer to these questions lies with the expectations of your audience. Although your only audience now may be your instructor, you will write more effective essays if you consider the needs of a larger audience, one that *includes* your instructor. Pretend, if you like, that you are publishing your essay in a magazine or journal whose audience contains many people who genuinely enjoy literature. You might want to personalize this audience by imagining that people you know are in it— friends, relatives, classmates. There are, by the way, many magazines and journals that address themselves to an audience that enjoys and reads literature regularly—*Saturday Review, The New York Times Book Review, The American Scholar, The New Republic, The Sewanee Review, Harper's, The Atlantic*. You might want to scan these to see how professional writers deal with their material and relate to their audience. You can assume that the members of your audience would take satisfaction in understanding literature better. Being intelligent and curious, they would raise questions about what they read and would want these questions answered. All in all, an important reason for writing essays about literature is to satisfy this desire of your audience to *know*.

There is, however, another reason for writing essays about literature. That reason is to satisfy your own needs and desires. Writing is not just the end product of thinking, it is a *way* of thinking. Some theorists argue that not until you write out your ideas can you be sure you have thought them through carefully. The process of writing essays, for example, underscores the need to use sound logic, to include all the steps in your reasoning, to state ideas precisely in order to produce arguments that will withstand the scrutiny of objective and intelligent people. It is easy *not* to do these things when you are just thinking to yourself or speaking to other people. Francis Bacon's maxim suggests this result of writing: "Reading maketh a full man, conference a ready man, and writing an exact man."

But perhaps the most important result of writing is its ability to draw forth your ideas. One kind of essay about literature is the essay examination (discussed in Chapter 11). You may find essay examinations burdensome and even traumatic, but in writing them students often discover ideas they never knew they had. That is, the writing process mates the students' knowledge of literature with the instructor's questions to give birth to new ideas. Essays about literature, then, can be journeys of self-discovery in which, as you write, you happen upon new intellectual vistas. In a sense, you are part of your audience. You share your readers' curiosity and their desire to have puzzling questions answered. You write to convince them, but you write also to discover and clarify your ideas and convince yourself of their validity.

WHAT MAKES AN ESSAY TOPIC "GOOD"?

Given that essay topics emerge from questions that curious readers raise about literature, when is a topic "good"? One way to judge the quality of an essay topic is to ask yourself how easily an average reader could answer the question that lies behind it. A useful guideline is that a topic is "good" if most readers could *not* answer the question after reading the work once. That is, readers could not answer it convincingly, either for themselves or for others, without reviewing and studying the work. The topic, in other words, is genuinely thought-provoking.

A second consideration is the meaningfulness of the topic. In order for a topic to be good, it should be worth considering. There is admittedly a subjective judgment involved here. Some readers may think a question worth answering, others not. But a topic is good if, in your judgment (and your instructor's!), answering the question would enhance your audience's understanding of the work. Perhaps, therefore, the most meaning*less* question is, What happened in the work? True, the events and details of a work sometimes are hard to understand and need clarification (in William Faulkner's or T. S. Eliot's writings, for example); but usually readers can understand a work's details after reading the work one time. There's no need to describe information merely for the sake of describing information.

A third way to assess the quality of a topic is to ask if it is focused narrowly enough for the confines of your essay. Most of the essays you write for college literature classes will run from three to ten typewritten pages (900 to 3,000 words). Your topic is good if you can deal with it thoroughly within those limits. For example, "comedy in *Romeo and Juliet*" would be too broad for an essay topic; "the nurse as comic figure" would be more specific and manageable. "Love in *Romeo and Juliet*" would be too broad; "Juliet's mature love versus Romeo's adolescent love" would be better. "Values in *Romeo and Juliet*"—too broad; "Shakespeare's attitude toward suicide"—better. "Juliet as character"—too broad; "Juliet's change from child to young woman"—better.

Charlotte Brontë's novel *Jane Eyre* provides us with an essay topic that meets all three criteria. Brontë grew up absorbing the superstitions of the English north country. These superstitions included beliefs in fairies, elves, and demons, and one doesn't have to read far into *Jane Eyre* before encountering references to them. Jane (the narrator and main character) tells us that as a child she looked for elves in vain "under mushrooms and beneath the ground-ivy" and concluded that "they were all gone out of England to some savage country where the woods were wilder and thicker, and the population more scant." After her first encounter with Mr. Rochester, he accuses her of being a fairy who "bewitched" his horse and caused it to fall. Her reply is that the fairies "all forsook England a hundred years ago." Throughout their relationship, he calls her "elf," "fairy," "dream," "changeling," "sprite." After she returns at the end of the novel, he reverts to his epithets, once again calling her "fairy," "ghost," "changeling," "fairy-born and human-bred." A topic for an essay about *Jane Eyre,* then, might be its use of fairy lore. The question underlying the topic would be, What significance does this lore have in the novel? The topic is meaningful because it is prominent in the work and is consistently associated with the main character; it promises to teach the reader a great deal about the novel. The topic, furthermore, is complex enough so that a reader could not answer its question fully and convincingly without going back through the novel and studying it. And the topic is specific enough to be dealt with thoroughly in an essay of about 1,200 to 1,500 words. The topic, in short, is "good."

THE LITERARY GENRES

A good essay topic, in summary, needs to be thought-provoking, meaningful, and narrowly focused. And it will almost always arise from searching questions you ask about individual works. How do you come up with such questions? Your own imaginative and creative response to literature is always one source of questions, and some people have this gift in greater abundance than others. But even very creative people must learn to control and channel their creativity; otherwise its products will often be superficial. To channel your creative response to literature, you need to learn to analyze it systematically and minutely. One way of doing so is to study the elements of literature. This chapter, then, begins an examination of the "genres" of literature. The word *genre* comes from French and means "type" or "kind." Literary critics sometimes disagree over what the genres are, but for a general approach to literature it is useful to consider three broad "kinds"—fiction, poetry, and drama. This chapter begins with the most popular genre, fiction.

You will find explanations of the genres in many other places—anthologies, handbooks to literature, encyclopedias, other textbooks. But the explanations in this book have two purposes: first, to provide definitions of the elements of each genre that you can refer to in all your literature courses; and, second, to provide you with a way to *think* about literature and thus to generate topics about it. After the discussions of the elements of each genre, we present questions that you can ask about these elements—questions that should produce a greater understanding of a given work and that should produce topics for essays about it.

THE NATURE OF FICTION

As a descriptive term, "fiction" is misleading, for although fiction does often include made-up or imaginary elements, it has the potential for being "true," true to the nature of reality, true to human experience. The intellectual activity that most resembles fiction is history. Both attempt to create a world that resembles the multiplicity and complexity of the real world. Both attempt to speculate about the nature of the real world. But fiction is different from history in key ways, and these differences help reveal the nature and uniqueness of fiction.

The most obvious difference is that writers of fiction can make up facts but that historians must take facts as they find them. In works of history, historians cannot manufacture facts to fill in the gaps of their knowledge. Consequently, the fictional world is potentially more complete and coherent than the historical world. Not only can writers of fiction produce facts at will, they can produce them to fit a coherent plan. If they have an optimistic view of reality, for example, they can include only positive and affirming facts. Furthermore, they can know more about their worlds than historians (or anyone else) can know about the real world. They can enter their characters' minds, look into the heavens, create chains of cause and effect, pierce the future. A second difference is that writers of fiction must establish some principle of order or coherence that underlies their work. They must establish at least an aesthetic order, and they may also impose a philosophical order upon their materials. Although historians often do both, they need do neither. Like newspaper reporters, historians need only record events as they occur, no matter how unrelated or senseless they may seem. A third difference is that writers of fiction must build conflict into their worlds, whereas historians need not. The events of history are not inevitably characterized by conflict, but the events of fiction always are.

All three of these differences point to qualities that make fiction innately enjoyable—its imaginative, orderly, and dramatic qualities. But two more differences reveal an equally important aspect of fiction—the kinds of reality it deals with and thus the kinds of truth it attempts to expose. The fourth difference, then, is that writers of fiction celebrate the separateness, distinctness, and importance of all individuals and all individual experiences. They assume that human experiences, whatever they are and wherever they occur, are intrinsically important and interesting. In contrast, historians record and celebrate human experiences that affect or represent large numbers of people—wars, rises and falls of civilizations, technological innovations, economic developments, political changes, social tastes and mores. If historians discuss individuals at all, it is because they affect or illustrate these wider experiences. Henry Fleming, the protagonist of Stephen Crane's novel *The Red Badge of Courage,* has no historical importance. As far as history is concerned, he is an anonymous participant in the Civil War battle of Chancellorsville, one of thousands. Even his deeds, thoughts, and feelings do not necessarily represent those of the typical soldier at Chancellorsville. Yet in the fictional world, they are important because they are *his* deeds, thoughts, and feelings. We are interested in him not for his connection with an important historical event but simply because he is a human being.

Finally, a fifth difference is that writers of fiction see reality as welded to psychological perception, as refracted through the minds of individuals. In contrast, historians present reality as external to individuals and thus as unaffected by human perception. Both historians and writers of fiction, for example, deal with time. But time for the historian is divisible into exact, measurable units—centuries, decades, years, months, weeks, days, hours, minutes, seconds. Time, for historians, is a river in which individuals float like so many pieces of driftwood. In contrast, writers of fiction present time as an experienced, emotional phenomenon, as a river flowing *inside* the mind. Its duration is not scientifically measurable but rather is determined by states of mind, the familiar when-I-am-happy-time-goes-fast, when-I-am-sad-time-goes-slow phenomenon. Other aspects of reality take on a similar psychological dimension within works of fiction. A house may not be haunted, but the character perceives it as such out of fear and anxiety. A mountain may not be steep, but the character perceives it as such out of fatigue and aching muscles.

THE ELEMENTS OF FICTION

This explanation of the nature of fiction should make you consciously aware of what generally to expect from it. However, fiction, poetry, and drama all have specific elements that exist from work to work. Some elements may be emphasized more than others, but all are potentially present in any given work. If you know what these elements are, you can break down a work into its components. That is, you can analyze it. The rest of this chapter, then, describes the elements of fiction and provides key questions for you to ask about the use of these elements in specific works.

Plot

Put simply, *plot* is what happens in a narrative. But this definition is too simple. A mere listing of events, even in the order in which they occur, is not plot. Rather, writers of fiction arrange fictional events into patterns, they select these events carefully, they establish causal relationships among events, and they enliven these events with conflict. A more complete and accurate definition, then, is that plot is a pattern of carefully selected, causally related events that contains conflict.

Although writers of fiction arrange events into many patterns, the most common is that represented by the Freytag pyramid shown here, which was developed by the German critic Gustav Freytag in 1863. Although Freytag meant this diagram to describe a typical five-act tragedy, it may be adapted to apply to most works of fiction. At the beginning of this pattern is an unstable situation, a conflict that sets the plot in motion. The author's exposition here involves an explanation of the nature of the conflict. He or she introduces the characters, describes the setting, and provides histor-

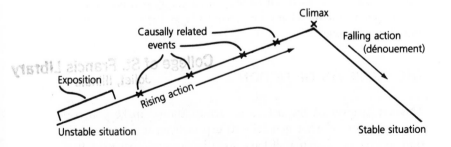

ical background. He or she then introduces a series of events, each of which causes the one that follows and each of which intensifies the conflict. As a result, the plot "rises" toward a climax. The climax is the most intense event in the narrative. The rest of the story—the falling action—is usually brief. It contains events that are much less intense than the climax and that lead toward the resolution of the conflict and toward a stable situation at the end. Another term for falling action is *dénouement,* a French word meaning "unravelling." An example of the Freytag pyramid is the stereotypical fairy tale in which the youngest son must seek his fortune (unstable situation: he has no source of income, no home). He goes into a far country whose king is offering a prize, the hand of his daughter for anyone who can accomplish three tasks. The hero successfully completes all three (rising action and climax: each task is increasingly difficult, but the third is a humdinger). The king praises the hero but does not want his daughter to marry a commoner. The hero reveals that he is not, as he seems, a mere peasant but the son of a nobleman (falling action/dénouement: the conflicts now are minor and easily resolved). The hero marries the princess and lives happily ever after (stable situation: the hero has eliminated the initial conflict; he now has a wife, a source of income, and a home).

There are two general categories of conflict, external and internal. Internal conflicts take place within the minds of characters. An example is the good person who wrestles inwardly with temptation. External conflicts take place between individuals or between individuals and the forces of nature. The climactic shootout in an American western is an example of a physical external conflict, but not all external conflicts are physical or violent. A disagreement between two people is also an external conflict.

The forces in a conflict are usually embodied by characters, the most relevant being the protagonist and the antagonist. The term *protagonist* usually means "main character," but it might be helpful sometimes to think of the protagonist as someone who is fighting for something. The *antagonist* is the opponent of the protagonist; the antagonist is usually an individual, but can also be a nonhuman force or even an aspect of the protagonist—his or her tendency toward evil and self-destruction, for example. Usually we empathize with the protagonist, whereas we find the antagonist unsympathetic.

Questions about plot   Probably the single most revealing question you can ask about a work of literature is, What conflicts does it dramatize? For fiction, this is a crucial question. You
can break it down into subquestions, each of which might produce
an interesting essay topic: What is the main conflict? What are the
minor conflicts? How are all the conflicts related? Which conflicts
are external, which internal? Who is the protagonist? What qualities
or values does the author associate with each side of the conflict?
How is the main conflict organized? How is it resolved? But the
overall question should be, simply, What are the important conflicts?

An example of how you can use this question to analyze fiction is Ernest Hemingway's story "Hills Like White Elephants."
The story consists almost entirely of a dialogue between a young
woman and man who are waiting for a train at a tiny station in the
Spanish countryside. We learn that they have traveled widely, that
they are intimate, that they are lovers. But they are in conflict.
About what? The conflict that they bring out into the open, discuss
out loud, concerns an abortion. The woman is pregnant, and the
man urges her to have an abortion. He keeps telling her that the
abortion will be "simple," "perfectly natural," and will make them
"all right" and "happy." But she resists. She asks if after the abortion "things will be like they were and you'll love me." She says
that they "could get along" without the abortion.

Gradually we realize that although the immediate conflict is
over the abortion, there is a deeper, unspoken conflict. This more
important conflict—the main conflict—is over the nature of their
relationship. The man wants the abortion because it will allow him
to continue the rootless and uncommitted relationship he has enjoyed with the woman up to now. The woman, however, wants a
more stable relationship, one that having the child would affirm,
one that she has apparently believed the man wanted too. Hemingway resolves the conflict by having the woman realize, in the face
of the man's continued insistence on the abortion, that the relationship she wants with the man is impossible.

Analyzing the story's conflict in this way helps to reveal several important things about it. At first glance, it seems to have little
"action," but analyzing the conflict reveals what its action is. Analyzing the conflict also helps to illuminate the characters: the man
is selfish and obstinate, the woman is idealistic and somewhat in-

nocent. And analyzing the conflict points to the meaning or theme of the story. Hemingway seems to support the woman's view of the way a loving relationship should be. He makes her the protagonist, the more sympathetic character of the two. Because analyzing conflict in works of literature is crucial to understanding them, such an analysis is a rich source of essay topics, perhaps the richest. This analysis of "Hills Like White Elephants" is but one of many examples of what an essay might do with conflict.

Characterization

Characters are the people in narratives, and characterization is the author's presentation and development of characters. Sometimes, as in fantasy fiction, the characters are not people. They may be animals, or robots, or creatures from outer space, but the author gives them human abilities and human psychological traits. Thus they really are people in all but outward form.

There are two broad categories of character development—simple and complex. The critic and fiction writer E. M. Forster coined alternate terms for these same categories—*flat* (simple) and *round* (complex) characters. Flat characters have only one or two personality traits and are easily recognizable as stereotypes—the shrewish wife, the lazy husband, the egomaniac, the stupid athlete, the shyster, the miser, the redneck, the bum, the dishonest used-car salesman, the prim aristocrat, the absent-minded professor. Round characters have multiple personality traits and therefore resemble real people. They are much harder to understand and describe than flat characters. No single description or interpretation can fully contain them. An example of a flat character is Washington Irving's Ichabod Crane, the vain and superstitious schoolmaster of "The Legend of Sleepy Hollow." An example of a round character is Shakespeare's Hamlet. To an extent all literary characters are stereotypes. Even Hamlet is a type, the "melancholy man." But round characters have many more traits than just those associated with their general type. Because it takes time to develop round characters convincingly, they are more often found in longer works than in shorter ones.

Authors reveal what characters are like in two general ways, directly or indirectly. In the direct method, the author simply tells the reader what the character is like. Here, for example, is Jane Austen telling us, very early in her novel *Pride and Prejudice,* what Mrs. Bennet is like:

> She was a woman of mean understanding, little information, and uncertain temper. When she was discontented she fancied herself nervous. The business of her life was to get her daughters married; its solace was visiting and news.

When the method of revealing characters is indirect, however, the author shows us, rather than tells us, what the characters are like through what they say about one another, through external details (dress, bearing, looks), through their thoughts, speech, and deeds.

Characters who remain the same throughout a work are called *static* characters. Characters who change in the course of the work are called *dynamic* characters. Usually, round characters change and flat characters remain the same. But not always. Shakespeare's Sir John Falstaff (in *Henry IV, Parts I and II*), a round character, is nonetheless static. Dynamic characters, especially main characters, typically grow in understanding. The climax of this growth is an *epiphany,* a term that James Joyce used to describe a sudden revelation of truth experienced by a character. The term comes from the Bible and describes the Wise Men's first perception of Christ's divinity. Joyce applied it to fictional characters. His own characters, like Gabriel Conroy in "The Dead," perfectly illustrate the concept. Often, as in "The Dead," the epiphany occurs at the climax of the plot.

Questions about characters   There are many questions you can ask about characters and the way they are portrayed: Are they flat, round, dynamic, or static? What do they learn? Does what they learn help or hinder them? What types do they represent? But the overriding questions that any character analysis attempts to answer are rather simple and obvious: What is the character like? What are his or her traits? An example is the woman in Hemingway's "Hills Like White Elephants," discussed above. Hemingway drops hints that indicate something about her personality. She compares the Spanish hills to white elephants, a comparison that at first seems capricious but later suggests an imaginative, even artistic quality that the man cannot comprehend. After she senses the man's true motivation for wanting the abortion, she looks out over the fields of ripe grain, the trees, the river, and the mountains beyond, and tells the man that "we could have all this" but that "every day we make it more impossible." She seems to connect the appreciation of nature, the sympathy they could feel for it, with the moral quality of their relationship. But because their relationship must remain superficial, she says that the landscape "isn't ours any more." Once again, the man lacks the imagination to make the connection, and he fails to grasp her moral point. Hemingway seems to admire the woman's ability to make these comparisons. It underscores her more obvious and admirable desire for a profound and lasting relationship. Another thing we learn about the woman is that she is a dynamic character. At the beginning of the story she doesn't fully recognize the falseness of her relationship with the man. She seems genuinely to hope for something better. But by the end of the story she knows the truth and, from all appearances, has changed as a result. At the beginning she is innocent and dependent on the man for her happiness; by the end she has lost her innocence and has become independent.

Theme

Theme is the central idea in a work—whether fiction, poetry, or drama. It is the comment the work makes on the human condition. It deals with four general areas of human experience: the nature of humanity, the nature of society, the nature of humankind's relationship to the world, and the nature of our ethical responsibilities. Theme answers questions like the following: Are human beings innately "sinful" or "good"? Does fate (environment, heredity, circumstance) control us or do we control it? What does a particular social system (capitalism, socialism, feudalism, totalitarianism, democracy, bureaucracy) do for—and to—its members?

You should distinguish between subject (or topic) and theme. The subject is what the work is about. You can state the subject in a word or phrase. The subject of Shakespeare's Sonnet 116 (see page 66 for the complete sonnet) is simply, "love." Theme is what the work says about the subject. The statement of a work's theme requires a complete sentence, or even several sentences. The theme of Sonnet 116 is, "Love remains constant whether assaulted by tempestuous events or by time."

For many readers, theme is an attractive element because it gives works meaning; it makes them relevant. But searching for theme has its pitfalls. To avoid them you should know several characteristics of theme in works of fiction. First, a work's theme must apply to people outside the work. For example, it is incorrect to say that the theme of "Rip Van Winkle" is, "Rapid change in his environment threatens Rip's identity." This statement is true but is not the theme, because it applies only to Rip. A more accurate statement of the theme would be, "Rapid change in environment causes many people to feel their identity threatened." In other words, stating theme in a work of literature is a process of abstraction. It involves moving from the concrete situations within the work to the general situations of people outside the work.

A second characteristic of theme is that many works have more than one subject and thus more than one theme. This is especially true of complex works. A subject of Tolstoy's *Anna Karenina* is clearly sacred versus profane love. But another, equally important subject is social entrapment. One theme of *Anna Karenina*, then, is that people should not abandon "sacred" commitments, like marriage and parenthood, for extramarital "loves," no matter how passionate and deeply felt they may be. This theme emerges from Anna's desertion of her husband and child for Count Vronsky. But an alternate theme is that people, through little fault of their own, can become trapped in painful, long-lasting, and destructive relationships that they want desperately to escape. This theme emerges from Anna's marriage. When she was very young, Anna married an older man whom she now realizes is too petty, prim, and self-absorbed to satisfy her generous and passionate nature. So discordant is her relationship with her husband that it seems no less "immoral" than her affair with Vronsky. Tolstoy, in other words, draws complex, even contradictory lessons from Anna's adultery. She is not simply the sinful person; she is also the driven person. And this combination of traits characterizes the condition of many people.

Third, some works may not have a subject or a theme. There may be so many contradictory or incompletely developed elements in a work that it is impossible to say for sure what the work means. Examples of such works are Edgar Allan Poe's "The Raven" and "The Fall of the House of Usher."

Fourth, the subject and theme of complex works can never be determined with complete certainty. Even when the author says what the work means, you cannot exclude other possibilities. To get at a work's theme, you must seek patterns in the concrete world the author creates. You must extrapolate from the evidence. But you can never see all the evidence at once or see all the possible patterns that are inherent in them. The best you can do is support your interpretations as logically and with as much evidence as you can. You may disagree with the author's conclusions about a given subject—with his or her theme. But your job is first to identify and understand the work's theme and then, if you are writing about it, to represent it fairly. To represent it fairly, however, is not necessarily to agree with it. You are always free, in your own mind, to disagree with an author's world view.

Questions about theme   The key questions for eliciting a work's theme are, What is the subject (that is, What is the work about)? What is the theme (that is, What does the work say about the subject)? In order to answer these questions (and support your answers with evidence), you need to answer another question: In what direct and indirect ways—plot, setting, characterization, and so on—does the work communicate its theme? In "Hills Like White Elephants," Hemingway doesn't state his subject and theme directly, but given his development of conflict and character (described above), it seems logical to conclude that his subject is "love" (or "loving relationships") and that his theme is something like the following: "Loving relationships are impossible without unselfish commitment from both partners."

Setting

Setting includes several closely related aspects of a work of fiction. First, setting is the physical, sensuous world of the work. Second, it is the time in which the action of the work takes place. And third, it is the social environment of the characters—the manners, customs, and moral values that govern the characters' society. A fourth aspect—"atmosphere"—is largely but not entirely an effect of setting.

Questions about place   You should first get the details of the physical setting clear in your mind. Where does the action take place? What sensuous qualities does the author give to the setting? Once you have answered these questions, you can move on to a more interesting one: What relationship does place have to characterization and theme? In some novels, geographical location seems to have no effect on characters. Indoors or out, in one locale or another, they behave the same. In other novels, like Thomas Hardy's or Joseph Conrad's, place affects the characters profoundly. Here is Hamlin Garland depicting the relationship of environment to the process of making decisions:

> A cornfield in July is a hot place. The soil is hot and dry; the wind comes across the lazily murmuring leaves laden with a warm sickening smell drawn from the rapidly growing, broad-flung banners of the corn. The sun, nearly vertical, drops a flood of dazzling light and heat upon the field over which the cool shadows run, only to make the heat seem the more intense.
>
> Julia Peterson, faint with fatigue, was toiling back and forth between the corn rows, holding the handles of the double-shovel corn plow while her little brother Otto rode the steaming horse. Her heart was full of bitterness, and her face flushed with heat, and her muscles aching with fatigue. The heat grew terrible. The corn came to her shoulders, and not a breath seemed to reach her, while the sun, nearing the noon mark, lay pitilessly upon her shoulders, protected only by a calico dress. The dust rose under her feet, and as she was wet with perspiration it soiled her till, with a woman's instinctive cleanliness, she shuddered. Her head throbbed dangerously. What matter to her that the king bird pitched jovially from the maples to catch a wandering bluebottle fly, that the robin was feeding its young, that the bobolink was singing? All these things, if she saw them, only threw her bondage to labor into greater relief.

In this story, "Among the Corn Rows," Garland shows geographical environment pressuring Julia Peterson into a decision that will affect the rest of her life. Garland has already told us that her parents treat her harshly and force her to work too hard. By emphasizing one sensuous quality, the heat, Garland makes us feel the hardship of her life. She dreams of a handsome, nonfarming suitor who will rescue her from this misery. Instead, she chooses to marry a young farmer who happens along just after the incident described above and who will afford her a life of respect and of only normal difficulty. Garland shows that Julia's environment forces her to settle for a less than ideal solution to her problems. She is not free to choose exactly as she would choose.

Questions about time   Three kinds of time occur in fiction, thus three questions are important. First, at what period in history does the action take place? Many stories occur during historical events that affect the characters in important ways. Margaret Mitchell's *Gone with the Wind* and Tolstoy's *War and Peace* are examples. Second, how long does it take for the action to occur? That is, how many hours, days, weeks, years are involved? Third, how is the passage of time perceived? Time may seem to move very slowly or very quickly, depending on a character's state of mind.

Charlotte Brontë's handling of time is a significant aspect of the setting of *Jane Eyre*. Although the novel's historical time is unimportant (the author makes no references to contemporary events), the length of time and perception of time are extremely important. Actually, Brontë closely relates the two. The length of time that Jane spends at the various "houses" in the novel gives structure to it; these stays constitute distinct episodes. Furthermore, the time Jane spends relating the episodes is directly proportional to the value she places on them. She devotes 97 pages (in the Penguin edition) to her stays with the Reeds and at Lowood (in her tenth year), 97 pages to her ten-month stay with the Rivers family, but 235 pages to her ten-month stay at Thornfield, where she falls in love with Mr. Rochester. The effect of these unequal proportions is to slow down the time spent at Thornfield and thus to emphasize Jane's emotional reaction to the experiences she has there.

Brontë uses this slowing-down method with specific events as well. In fact, the novel is a collection of highly charged, intensely felt moments in Jane's life that seem to last far longer than they actually do. The novel opens, for example, with Jane's imprisonment in the hated "red room" of the Reed mansion. As her anger subsides, she becomes aware that the room is "chill," "silent," and "solemn." She recalls that Mr. Reed died there. In a mirror she sees her "glittering eyes of fear moving where all else was still." Daylight "forsakes" the room. She feels "oppressed, suffocated" at thoughts of Mr. Reed's death and the possibility of her own. When she sees a light on the wall, she thinks it is a ghost. She screams. Mrs. Reed rushes to check on her. She thrusts Jane back into the room and locks the door. Jane faints from hysteria. The length of this description corresponds to Jane's perception of time, which in turn corresponds to her fear of the room. Each detail is like the tick of a loud clock.

Questions about social environment   Often the social environment represented in a work is of little importance. Sometimes, in fact, there is virtually no social environment. But when it seems important, a good essay topic should emerge from this question: How do the manners, mores, and customs portrayed in the work affect the characters? Sinclair Lewis spends much of his novel *Babbitt* describing the social environment of his fictional midwestern city, Zenith. And then he shows that the pressure to conform to this environment is almost irresistible. His characters sometimes want to rebel against this pressure, but they are too weak to do so without extreme guilt or without threat to their economic and social security. Their social environment determines their behavior and entraps them.

Questions about atmosphere   *Atmosphere* refers to the emotional reaction that we and—usually—the characters have to the setting of a work. Sometimes the atmosphere is difficult to define, but it often inheres in the sensuous quality of the setting. Our emotional reaction to the Hamlin Garland passage above is pain, discomfort, weariness, and oppression, mainly because of his emphasis on the thermal sense, the sense of hot and cold. Your most fruitful questions about atmosphere will probably be, What is the atmosphere? and What does the author achieve by creating this atmosphere? Sometimes, the author's purpose may simply be to play upon your emotions (Poe, for example, wants to scare us). Garland's purpose, however, is more serious. He seems to want to convince us of a philosophical point: physical environment affects human behavior.

Point of view

Point of view is the author's relationship to his or her fictional world, especially to the minds of the characters. Another way of putting this is to define point of view as the position from which the story gets told. There are four common points of view, four positions the author can adopt as he or she tells the story.

Omniscient point of view   In the omniscient position, the author, not one of the characters, tells the story, and the author assumes complete knowledge of the characters' actions and thoughts. The author can thus move at will from one place to another, one time to another, one character to another, and can even speak his or her own views directly to the reader as the work goes along. The author will tell us anything he or she chooses about the created world of the work. Many of the great eighteenth- and nineteenth-century novels utilize an omniscient point of view; examples are Hawthorne's *The Scarlet Letter,* Hardy's *Tess of the D'Urbervilles,* and Fielding's *Joseph Andrews.*

Limited omniscient point of view   When the limited omniscient position is used, the author still narrates the story but restricts (limits) his or her revelation—and therefore our knowledge—of the thoughts of all but one character. This character may be either a main or peripheral character. A device of plot and characterization that often accompanies this point of view is the character's gradual discovery of himself or herself until the story climaxes in an epiphany (see "Characterization," above). Examples of the limited omniscient point of view are Hawthorne's "Young Goodman Brown," James Joyce's "Araby," and, for the most part, Jane Austen's *Pride and Prejudice.* Sometimes the author restricts the point of view so severely that we see everything solely through the mind of a single character, like sunlight filtered through the leaves and branches of a tall tree. The later fiction of Henry James experiments with this severe restriction of the limited omniscient point of view. His story "The Beast in the Jungle" and his novel *The Ambassadors* are examples. Other writers, like James Joyce, Virginia Woolf, and William Faulkner, followed up on James's experiments with a "stream of consciousness" technique, which puts the reader literally in the mind of a character. In the first section of Faulkner's *The Sound and the Fury* we experience the chaotic thoughts of a mentally retarded man, and we view the novel's world solely through his mind.

First-person point of view   In the first-person position, the author is even more restricted: one of the characters tells the story, eliminating the author as narrator. Whereas in the limited omniscient point of view the author can reveal anything about one character, even things the character may be dimly aware of, here the narration is restricted to what one character *says* he or she observes. The character/narrator may be a major character who is at the center of events or a minor character who does not participate but simply observes the action. Examples of first-person narratives are Dickens' *Great Expectations,* Twain's *Huckleberry Finn,* Robert Penn Warren's *All the King's Men,* and F. Scott Fitzgerald's *The Great Gatsby.*

Objective (dramatic) point of view   In the objective position, the author is more restricted than in any other. Though the author is the narrator, he or she refuses to enter the minds of any of the characters. The writer sees them (and lets us see them) as we would in real life. This point of view is sometimes called "dramatic" because we see the characters as we would the characters in a play. We learn about them from what they say and do, how they look, and what other characters say about them. But we don't learn what they think unless they tell us. This point of view is the least common of all. Examples are Hemingway's "Hills Like White Elephants" and "The Killers" and Stephen Crane's "The Blue Hotel."

Tone   *Tone* is also an aspect of point of view since it has a great deal to do with the narrator. Tone is the narrator's predominant attitude toward the subject, whether that be a particular setting, an event, a character, an idea. The narrator conveys his or her attitude through the way narrative devices are handled, including choice of words. Sometimes the narrator will state point-blank how he or she feels about a subject; more often, the narrator's attitude is conveyed indirectly. Jack Burden, the narrator of Warren's *All the King's Men,* maintains a flippant and cynical tone through most of the narration. Jake Barnes, the narrator of Hemingway's *The Sun Also Rises,* maintains a stoical, hardboiled tone. Dr. Watson, the narrator of the Sherlock Holmes stories, manifests a bemused, surprised tone.

Questions about point of view   Point of view is important to an understanding of a story in two main ways. First, the author may choose a particular point of view in order to emphasize one character's perception of things. The omniscient narrator can tell us what a character thinks, but the limited omniscient and first-person points of view make us *experience* what the character thinks. To make the emphasis even more emphatic, an author may include several points of view in the same work. Dickens in *Bleak House* shuttles back and forth between a first-person narrative and an omniscient narrative. We see that the first-person narrator has a more limited view of things than the omniscient narrator. Point of view here becomes a means of developing character and of making a point about the limits of human perception. Once you have determined a work's point of view, a good essay topic might emerge from this question: Why has the author chosen it? What effects, that is, does it have on other elements of the story—theme, characterization, setting, language?

Second, point of view is important when you suspect the trustworthiness of the narrator. A preliminary question is, Who tells the story? But a searching follow-up question is, Can you trust the narrator? You can almost always trust omniscient narrators. But you should be suspicious about first-person narrators and the "centers-of-consciousness" characters in limited omniscient stories. Sometimes these characters distort what they observe. Ask, then, if certain circumstances, like their age, education, social status, prejudices, or emotional states, are such as to make you question the accuracy or validity of what they say and think. Ask, also, if the author differentiates between his or her view of things and the characters' view.

Mark Twain makes such a distinction in *Huckleberry Finn.*

When Huck sees the Grangerford house, he says, "It was a mighty nice family, and a mighty nice house, too. I hadn't seen no house out in the country before that was so nice and had so much style." He proceeds to describe the interior with awe and reverence. But although Huck is impressed with the furnishings, Twain clearly is not. We recognize Twain's attitude from the details Huck provides—the unread books, the reproductions of sentimental paintings, the damaged imitation fruit, the crockery animals, the broken clock, the painted hearth, the tablecloth "made out of beautiful oil-cloth," the piano "that had tin pans in it." Huck also shows his admiration for Emmeline Grangerford's poetry by reproducing some of it to share with us. But we see, as Twain wants us to see, that the poetry is mawkish and poorly written. Thus when Huck makes the following comment, he means one thing by it, while Twain means something quite different: "If Emmeline Grangerford could make poetry like that before she was fourteen, there ain't no telling what she could a done by-and-by." Finally, Huck is awe-struck by the family's aristocratic bearing: "Col. Grangerford was a gentleman, you see. He was a gentleman all over; and so was his family. He was well born. . . . He didn't have to tell anybody to mind their manners—everybody was always good mannered where he was." Yet he fails to see, as Twain sees and as we see, the ironic contrast between the family's good manners and its conduct of an illogical, murderous feud with another family. Twain's handling of point of view in this novel helps to develop both character and theme. By presenting Huck's benign and credulous view of things, it develops Huck as an essentially innocent person. By ironically contrasting Twain's view to Huck's, it underscores the author's harsher and more pessimistic perception of "reality."

Irony

Authors use irony pervasively to convey their ideas. But it is a diverse and often complex intellectual phenomenon difficult to define in a sentence or two. Generally, *irony* makes visible a contrast between appearance and reality. More fully and specifically, it exposes and underscores a contrast between what is and what seems to be, between what is and what ought to be, between what is and what one wishes to be, between what is and what one expects to be.

Incongruity is the method of irony; opposites come suddenly together so that the disparity is obvious to discriminating readers. There are many kinds of irony, but four are common in literature.

Verbal irony   Verbal irony is perhaps the most common form of irony. Most people use or hear verbal irony daily. In verbal irony, people say the opposite of what they mean. For example, if the day has been terrible, you might say, "Boy, this has been a great day!" The hearer knows that this statement is ironic because of the speaker's tone of voice and facial or bodily expressions or because the hearer is familiar with the situation and immediately sees the discrepancy between statement and actuality. Understatement and overstatement are two forms of verbal irony. In *understatement,* one minimizes the nature of something. "It was a pretty good game," one might say after seeing a no-hitter. Mark Twain's famous telegram is another example of understatement: "The reports of my death are greatly exaggerated." In *overstatement* one exaggerates the nature of something. After standing in a long line, you might say, "There were about a million people in that line!"

Why do people use verbal irony? The answer is that verbal irony is more emphatic than a point-blank statement of the truth. It achieves its effect by reminding the hearer or reader of what the opposite reality is and thus providing a scale by which to judge the present reality. Verbal irony also often represents a mental agility—wit—that people find striking and, as with the Mark Twain retort, entertaining. Verbal irony in its most bitter and destructive form becomes *sarcasm,* in which the speaker condemns someone by pretending to praise him:

> Oh, you're a real angel. You're the noble and upright man who wouldn't think of dirtying his pure little hands with company business. But all along, behind our backs, you were just as greedy and ruthless as the rest of us.

Situational irony   In situational irony, the situation is different from what common sense indicates it is, will be, or ought to be. It is ironic, for example, that General George Patton should have lived through the thickest of tank battles during World War II and then, after the war, have been killed accidentally by one of his own men. It is ironic that someone we expect to be upright—a minister or judge—should be the most repulsive of scoundrels. Authors often use situational irony to expose hypocrisy and injustice. A profound example is Hawthorne's *The Scarlet Letter,* in which the townspeople regard the minister Arthur Dimmesdale as sanctified and angelic when in fact he shamefully hides his adultery with Hester Prynne, allowing her to take all the blame.

Attitudinal irony Situational irony results from what *most* people expect, whereas attitudinal irony results from what one person expects. In attitudinal irony, an individual thinks that reality is one way when, in fact, it is a very different way. A frequent example in literature is the naïve character—Fielding's Parson Adams, Cervantes' Don Quixote, Dickens' Mr. Micawber, Voltaire's Candide—who thinks that everyone is upright and that everything will turn out for the best, when in fact the people they meet are consistently corrupt and the things that happen to them are destructive and painful.

Dramatic irony Dramatic irony occurs in plays when characters state something that they believe to be true but that the audience knows to be false. An example is the play *Oedipus Rex.* Like all Greek tragedies, *Oedipus Rex* dramatizes a myth that its audiences knew. Thus when Oedipus at the beginning boasts that he will personally find and punish the reprobate who killed King Laius, the audience recognizes this boast as ironic. Oedipus does not know, but the audience knows, that he himself is the unwitting murderer of Laius. Although dramatic irony gets its name from drama, it can occur in all forms of literature. The key to the existence of dramatic irony is the reader's foreknowledge of coming events. Many works become newly interesting when you reread them, because you now know what will happen but the characters do not; this dramatic irony intensifies characterization and makes you aware of tensions that you could not have known about during your initial reading.

Questions about irony The first question to ask is, What are the most obvious ironies in the work? The second is, How are the ironies important? What, for example, are their implications? Shirley Jackson's "The Lottery" is layered with irony. An essay might deal with one of its ironies, such as the ironic contrast between the placid country-town setting and the horrible deeds done there. The setting is everyone's nostalgic image of the ideal American small town, with its central square, post office, country store, cranky old men, gossipy housewives, laconic farmers, mischievous children, settled routine, and friendly atmosphere. Is Jackson implying, then, that "normal" American communities conduct lotteries to decide which of their members is to be destroyed by the others? The answer is yes, she is suggesting just this. Americans are guilty of conducting "lotteries," perhaps not exactly in this manner, but with equal arbitrariness and cruelty. Instead of making this point directly, however, she implies it through the use of irony. And she achieves a much greater emphasis than if she were to state her accusation directly. She shocks us by associating something that we all agree is horrible with a way of life that up to now we had thought was "normal" and benign. The irony packs an emotional wallop that at least gets our attention and, she hopes, will get us thinking.

Symbolism

In the broadest sense, a symbol is something that represents something else. Words, for example, are symbols. But in literature, a *symbol* is an object that has meaning beyond itself. The object is concrete and the meanings are abstract. Fire, for example, may symbolize general destruction (as in James Baldwin's title *The Fire Next Time*), or passion (the "flames of desire"), or hell (the "fiery furnace"). Symbols, however, are not metaphors; they are not analogies that clarify abstractions, like the following metaphor from Shakespeare's Sonnet 116: love

> is an ever-fixèd mark,
> That looks on tempests and is never shaken.

Here, the abstract concept (the referent) is "love" and the clarifying concrete object is the stable mark (buoy, lighthouse, rock) that tempests cannot budge. A symbol, in contrast, is a concrete object with no clear referent and thus no fixed meaning. Instead, it merely suggests the meaning and, in an odd way, partly *is* the meaning. For this reason, the meaning of symbols is difficult to pin down. And the more inexhaustible their potential meaning, the richer they are.

There are two kinds of symbol, public and private. Public (conventional) symbols are those that most people would recognize as meaning something fairly definite. Examples of public symbols are the cross, the star of David, and flags of countries. Private symbols are unique to an individual or to a single work. Only from clues in the work itself can we learn the symbolic value of the object. There are many examples of private symbols in literature. In F. Scott Fitzgerald's *The Great Gatsby,* there is an area between the posh Long Island suburbs and New York City through which the major characters drive at various times and which Fitzgerald calls a "valley of ashes." It is a desolate, grey, sterile place, and over it all broods a partly obliterated billboard advertisement that features the enormous eyes of Doctor T. J. Eckleburg, an optometrist. Fitzgerald invests this area with symbolic meaning. He associates it with moral decay, urban blight, the oppression of the poor by the wealthy, meaninglessness, hell, and violent death. At one point he connects the eyes with failure of vision, at another with God, who sees all things. But we never know exactly what the valley of ashes represents; instead it resonates with many possible meanings, and this resonance accounts for its powerful impact on readers.

Questions about symbolism   Not every work uses symbols, and not every character, incident, or object in a work has symbolic value. You should ask the fundamental question, What symbols does the work seem to have? But you should beware of finding "symbols" where none were intended. A second question, then, is necessary to the believability of any essay you might write on symbols: How do you know they are symbols? Or, What does the author do that gives symbolic meaning to the elements you mention? Once you answer this question to your own—and your reader's—satisfaction, you can move on to a third and more interesting question: What does the symbol mean? You could, for example, write about the symbolic meaning of rain in Hemingway's *A Farewell to Arms*. The following dialogue between Frederic Henry and Catherine Barkley strongly suggests that Hemingway intended a symbolic meaning for rain; it also suggests what the symbol represents:

> "It's raining hard." [Frederic says]
> "And you'll always love me, won't you?" [Catherine replies]

> "Yes."
>
> "And the rain won't make any difference?"
>
> "No."
>
> "That's good. Because I'm afraid of the rain."
>
> "Why? . . . Tell me."
>
> "All right. I'm afraid of the rain because sometimes I see me dead in it."
>
> "No."
>
> "And sometimes I see you dead in it. . . . It's all nonsense. It's only nonsense. I'm not afraid of the rain. I'm not afraid of the rain. Oh, oh, God, I wish I wasn't." She was crying. I comforted her and she stopped crying. But outside it kept on raining.

Hemingway's recurrent and consistent association of rain with destruction of all kinds broadens its significance from a mere metaphor for death to other and more general qualities, such as war, fate, alienation, foreboding, doom, "reality." Because of these associations, the last sentence of the novel is more than just a description of the weather: "After a while I went out and left the hospital and walked back to the hotel in the rain." The sentence seems to suggest that Frederic is stoically and bravely facing the harsh realities—including Catherine's death, the war, the arbitrariness and cruelty of fate—represented by the rain.

FOR FURTHER STUDY

Allen, Walter. *Reading a Novel*. London: Phoenix House, 1963.

Booth, Wayne C. *The Rhetoric of Fiction*. Chicago: Univ. of Chicago Press, 1961.

Forster, E. M. *Aspects of the Novel*. New York: Harcourt Brace Jovanovich, 1954.

Stevick, Philip, ed. *The Theory of the Novel*. New York: The Free Press, 1967.

Wellek, René, and Austin Warren. *Theory of Literature*. New York: Harcourt Brace Jovanovich, 1956.

Walter Allen's *Reading a Novel* is a brief introduction to the analysis of fiction; Allen is a literary historian and novelist. Wayne C. Booth in *The Rhetoric of Fiction* makes many cogent comments about the nature of fiction at the same time that he argues a thesis. His thesis is that fiction is rhetorical—that it offers comments on the nature of reality and uses various devices to persuade us that these comments are valid. E. M. Forster was an important twentieth-century English novelist, and his *Aspects of the Novel* is a beautifully written, compelling defense of what he thinks constitutes good fiction. In this book Forster coins and explains the terms "flat" and "round" characters, but he does much more. *The Theory of the Novel* is a collection of essays and excerpts; it tries to represent some of the best thinking on all the elements of fiction. Wellek and Warren's *Theory of Literature* is a difficult but brilliant book about the nature of literature; it discusses all the genres but is especially good on fiction. It has greatly influenced the discussion of literature in this book.

4

How to generate topics about drama and poetry

THE THREE GENRES—fiction, drama, and poetry—are different from one another, but they also share many of the same elements. They share, of course, all of the traits characteristic of "literature," described in Chapter 2. And they share more specific elements as well. This chapter focuses on those qualities that make drama and poetry different from fiction (thus the briefer treatment of drama and poetry and the placing of them both in this one chapter). Here, then, are definitions of the elements of the two genres and further questions for analyzing works and developing topics about them.

THE ELEMENTS OF DRAMA

Although very much like fiction, drama is different for one obvious reason—it is meant to be performed. The definitions and questions stated in Chapter 3 for plot, characterization, theme, setting, irony, and symbolism are all equally valid for drama. But because of the special nature of drama, portions of these definitions are more applicable than others, and questions inapplicable to fiction are revealing about drama. In this section we will review some of these differences and questions.

Characterization

Because the playwright has less time (only two hours or so) than the novelist to develop characters and because the playwright's audience experiences the play in one sitting, without an immediate opportunity to review it, he or she must present characters more simply and directly than the novelist. He or she must rely heavily, for example, on flat, stereotyped ("stock") characters, whose personalities and moral traits are readily recognizable by the audience. He or she may even use blatant devices, like dress, dialect, physical movements, and names, to communicate these traits. In Restoration and eighteenth-century drama, for example, playwrights used names to let audiences know what to expect even before the characters appeared onstage—names like Mrs. Loveit, Sir Fopling Flutter, Snake, Lady Teazle, Pert, Mr. Oldcastle, Lady Wishforit, Sneerwell, Smirk, Handy.

The playwright also must rely on static characters more heavily than upon dynamic characters. Restricted performance time limits the playwright's opportunity to make plausible the change that dynamic characters undergo. Macbeth and Othello are dynamic characters, but it is implausible that both of these essentially good men should become moral monsters in just a couple of hours. Only Shakespeare's art tricks us into accepting such character changes, but our acceptance is more emotional than intellectual, and it occurs more readily during performances than in readings of the plays.

The playwright, furthermore, is much more restricted than the novelist in the means available to reveal characters. Although the playwright can rely to some degree on exterior details (appearance, facial expressions, actions), the most important device is dialogue—what the character says and what other characters say about that character. Sometimes, to prepare us for a complex or powerful character, the playwright will let other characters talk about the character for a long time before the character appears. We don't meet Célèmine in Molière's *The Misanthrope* until the second act, but by then we have learned a great deal about her.

Another aspect of characterization unique to drama is the interpretation and presentation of characters by actors. In fact, the presence of real people in the guise of characters goes a long way toward creating the illusion that the characters, no matter how stereotyped or implausibly dynamic, are real and believable. The actor's craft and charisma can enliven good drama and transcend bad. Furthermore, actors can change significantly the way an audience perceives a character—by the way they inflect their voices, move around the stage, control the rate of their speech, use facial expressions, project their own personalities. An actor can make Hamlet seem like a suicidal maniac by rendering the "To be or not to be" speech with agony and despair, or he can make him a nonchalant, amateur philosopher by casually tossing off that soliloquy.

Questions about characters   The important questions you ask about characters in fiction are the same as those you ask about characters in plays. But you should give special attention to the kinds of characters the playwright uses and how he or she uses them. How are flat characters used to create conflict and develop theme? What characterizes the round characters? Do any of the characters change? How and why? A personal question is, How would *you* act a certain character? To answer this question, you would need to consider alternative "readings" of specific passages and scenes, and your choices would have to add up to a single, unified conception of the character.

Plot

As with characterization, the playwright must keep the plot simple and clear enough for an audience to grasp at one sitting. One advantage the playwright has over the novelist is that the playwright can present physical action without having to use words; this device is a timesaver, because it takes much less time for actors to perform actions than for a writer to describe them. But the actions and conflicts must be understandable, and almost the only means the playwright has of making them so is dialogue. In other words, every speech must somehow establish conflict and move the plot forward. Furthermore, the playwright must place greater emphasis on conflict than the novelist; the playwright must avoid lengthy descriptions of setting and characters, except in stage directions, which the audience does not see.

Another characteristic of drama—its structural divisions into acts and scenes—also affects plot. Playwrights usually provide structural divisions to give playgoers physical relief—a few moments to stand up, walk about, stretch, or even reflect on what they have seen. Structural divisions also serve to allow set changes. In addition to such performance considerations, however, structural divisions can mark off clearly defined segments of the plot. In some plays, each act is its own little drama, containing rising action that leads to a climax.

Questions about plot   Again, the key questions for plot in drama are the same as those for fiction. But in drama, structural divisions are more obvious and thus often deserve more attention than in fiction. What, for example, might a particular segment of the play (a scene or an act) contribute to the whole? How is the segment itself structured? Does it have its own rising action, climax, and dénouement? Also, drama depends more heavily than fiction on interactions between characters to develop conflict. Major verbal exchanges between characters always move the plot along and could in themselves be fruitful subjects for essays.

Setting

The setting of a play includes all its sensuous aspects—costumes, lighting, sets, movement (choreography), music—as well as the geographical location of the actions. The uniqueness of drama as a performed genre of fiction is perhaps most obvious when it comes to setting. Playwrights are limited by the demands of the place where a play is performed. They are limited in the number of characters they can put on the stage. They are limited in the geographical area they can represent by the stage. Furthermore, although a playwright may provide stage directions, describe stage properties, and envision characters' physical features, the director can ignore these ideas altogether.

However, the playwright—or at least the play's producer—has some tremendous advantages over the novelist in presenting setting. First, as with physical action, the sensuous experience of setting is immediately available to the audience. One glance at the stage by the audience will take in what might take the novelist hundreds of words to convey to readers. Second, setting can provide for the occurrence of simultaneous events. In Richard Brinsley Sheridan's *School for Scandal,* for example, one character hides behind a screen where she can hear other characters, who are unaware of her presence. If the stage is arranged properly, the audience sees her reactions to the overheard conversations. Or in *Death of a Salesman,* Arthur Miller calls for a house with two stories. Because the walls are cut away, the audience sees simultaneous action and hears simultaneous dialogue from both stories. Third, the playwright can draw upon other art forms to enhance the play and sometimes to express interpretations of the material. The most obvious extraliterary art form found in plays is visual—the way the stage is constructed and decorated and the way the characters look—and it can profoundly affect the audience's perception of the spoken material. Two more art forms sometimes incorporated into setting are music (as in musicals and opera) and dance.

Questions about setting   Two questions arise from different approaches to setting in drama. First, what does the playwright indicate about the setting through dialogue? Shakespeare continually has his characters compare Hamlet's Denmark to an unweeded garden. Setting, then, takes on substance for the reader or playgoer from the way the characters react to it or feel about it. Second, how might a production of the play present setting? Ideally, a production emphasizes the qualities of setting hinted or stated by the characters. Sometimes playwrights will specify the setting they want. Here is Eugene O'Neill describing his requirements for the firemen's forecastle of a transatlantic ship in the opening scene of *The Hairy Ape:*

> The effect sought after is a cramped space in the bowels of a ship, imprisoned by white steel. The lines of bunks, the uprights supporting them, cross each other like the steel framework of a cage. The ceiling crushes down upon the men's heads. They cannot stand upright. This accentuates the natural stooping posture which shoveling coal and the resultant over-development of back and shoulder muscles have given them. The men themselves should resemble those pictures in which the appearance of Neanderthal Man is guessed at.

A follow-up question is, Why does the playwright or the director call for such a setting? In *The Hairy Ape* O'Neill uses the setting to emphasize the thwarted and undeveloped human qualities of his protagonist, Yank, and of the exploited working class in general. He shows that all of capitalistic society is just as prisonlike for Yank and his fellow workers as the firemen's forecastle. A more personal question is, What kind of setting would *you* devise for the play?

Point of view

The playwright can modify or depart from the objective or dramatic point of view (described in Chapter 3, page 38) in only a few ways. One way is to tell you what a character thinks through devices like the soliloquy (in which the character "thinks out loud" while alone on the stage) and the aside (in which the character speaks directly to the audience). Another is to reveal a character's thoughts by having him or her speak them to a confidant. Another is to have one character, like the stage manager in Thornton Wilder's *Our Town,* take on the role of first-person narrator or commentator. Still another is to reveal his or her own views through nonverbal devices like setting and music. But by and large, the playwright's means of offering authorial comment or of revealing the minds of the characters during a performance are limited.

Questions about point of view   One goal in analyzing plays, then, is to ask what the playwright or producer *does* reveal about the characters, given these limitations. Perhaps the most important questions about point of view arise when the author departs from or modifies the objective point of view. In *The Emperor Jones,* Eugene O'Neill renders the protagonist's dreams and memories visually, and the increasingly fast and loud beating of the drums represents the character's growing apprehension. In *Strange Interlude,* O'Neill has the characters speak conscious thoughts out loud. These expressions are not quite asides and not quite soliloquies, because the characters do not speak directly to the audience and because the other characters cannot "hear" them. The audience hears them, of course, and thus not only learns more about the characters but sees the ironic difference between their thoughts and their statements.

POETRY

Poetry shares many elements with its sister genres, drama and fiction. And, indeed, many works of drama and fiction are written in the form of poetry. Plays by Shakespeare, Goethe, Molière, Marlowe, Maxwell Anderson, and T. S. Eliot; narrative works by Homer, Chaucer, Dante, Longfellow, Whittier, Jeffers, Milton, Spenser, Tennyson, and Browning are examples. But poetry is usually different from prose drama and fiction in several key ways. In general, it is more concentrated—that is, poetry says more in fewer words. Poets achieve this concentration by selecting details more carefully, by relying more heavily on implication (through figurative language, connotation, and sensuous imagery), and by more carefully organizing the form of their poetry (through rhythmic speech patterns and "musical" qualities, like rhyme). Because of the relative shortness of poetry and because of its greater concentration, it demands a more complete unity than prose fiction; every word, every sound, every image must work toward a single effect. The result is that poetry is more intense than the other genres.

Poetry is a complex subject. The following is a *brief* survey of its elements and questions about them that should lead you to good topics for essays on poetry.

Characterization, point of view, plot, and setting

Some poems—"narrative" poems—are very similar to prose fiction and drama in their handling of characterization, point of view, plot, and setting. Thus many of the same questions that one asks about a short story, novel, or play are relevant to these poems. Most poems, however, do not offer a "story" in the conventional sense. They are usually brief and apparently devoid of "action." Even so, a plot of sorts may be implied, a place and time may be important, a specific point of view may be operating, and characters may be dramatizing the key issues of the poem. In any poem there is always one "character" of the utmost importance, even if he or she is the only character. This character is the speaker, the "I" of the poem. Often the speaker is a fictional personage, not at all equivalent to the poet, and may not be speaking to the reader but to another character, as is the case in Marvell's "To His Coy Mistress" and Browning's "My Last Duchess." The poem might even be a dialogue between two or more people, as in ballads like "Edward" and "Lord Randal" and in Frost's "The Death of the Hired Man." Thus the poem can be a little drama or story, in which one or more fictional characters participates. But more typically, one character, the "I," speaks of something that concerns him or her deeply and personally. Such poems are called "lyric" poems because of their subjective, musical, highly emotional, and imaginative qualities. They are songlike utterances by one person, the "I."

Questions about characterization, point of view, plot, and setting   In analyzing poetry, your first step should be to come to grips with the "I" of the poem, the speaker. You should answer questions like these: Who is speaking? What characterizes the speaker? To whom is he or she speaking? What is his or her tone? Why is he or she speaking? What situation is being described? What are the conflicts or tensions in this situation? How is setting—time and place—important to the speaker?

Matthew Arnold's "Dover Beach" provides an example of how you could use most of these questions to get at the central meaning of a poem.

DOVER BEACH

MATTHEW ARNOLD

The sea is calm to-night.
The tide is full, the moon lies fair
Upon the straits; on the French coast the light
Gleams and is gone; the cliffs of England stand,
Glimmering and vast, out in the tranquil bay.
Come to the window, sweet is the night-air!
Only, from the long line of spray
Where the sea meets the moon-blanched land,
Listen! you hear the grating roar
Of pebbles which the waves draw back, and fling,
At their return, up the high strand,
Begin, and cease, and then again begin,

With tremulous cadence slow, and bring
The eternal note of sadness in.

Sophocles long ago
Heard it on the Aegean, and it brought
Into his mind the turbid ebb and flow
Of human misery; we
Find also in the sound a thought,
Hearing it by this distant northern sea.

The Sea of Faith
Was once, too, at the full, and round earth's shore
Lay like the folds of a bright girdle furled.
But now I only hear
Its melancholy, long, withdrawing roar,
Retreating, to the breath
Of the night-wind, down the vast edges drear
And naked shingles° of the world.

Ah, love, let us be true
To one another! for the world, which seems
To lie before us like a land of dreams,
So various, so beautiful, so new,
Hath really neither joy, nor love, nor light,
Nor certitude, nor peace, nor help for pain;
And we are here as on a darkling plain
Swept with confused alarms of struggle and flight,
Where ignorant armies clash by night.

°beaches covered with pebbles

Since Dover is an English port city, one of several points of departure for the continent, the speaker has apparently stopped for the night on his way to Europe. As he looks out of his hotel window, he speaks to another person in the room, his "love" (last stanza). Arnold traces the speaker's train of thought in four stanzas. In the first stanza, the speaker describes what he sees, and his tone is contented, even joyous. He sees the lights on the French coast, and he sees the high white cliffs of Dover "glimmering" in the moonlight. He invites his companion to share the glorious view. But as he describes the sound of the surf to her, his tone alters slightly; the sound reminds him of "the eternal note of sadness."

This melancholy tone deepens in the second stanza. There the speaker connects the sea sound with a passage in Sophocles, probably the third chorus of *Antigone,* which compares the misery of living under a family curse to the incessant roar of a stormy sea beating against the land.

In the third stanza, the remembrance of Sophocles' comparison leads the speaker to make a more disturbing comparison of his own. He likens the sea to faith—apparently religious faith, both his own and his age's. He says that at one time the "Sea of Faith" was full but now has withdrawn, leaving a "vast," "drear," and coarse world. By the fourth stanza, the speaker has fallen into despair. He says that what merely looks beautiful—the panorama seen from his window—is but a false image of the world, which in reality is absurd and chaotic. He has only one hope, his companion, whom he now urges to be true to him as he is true to her. The speaker, in short, is an erudite, thoughtful, but deeply troubled person. The poem takes him from momentary contentedness to near hopelessness. The stimulus for his train of thought is the place of the poem—Dover Beach—and the companion to whom he addresses his remarks. All these elements—thoughts, place, and companion—are interrelated.

Diction

Basically, *diction* refers to the poet's choice of words. Poets are sensitive to the subtle shades of meanings of words, to the possible double meanings of words, and to the denotative and connotative meanings of words. As we saw in Chapter 3, *denotation* is the object or idea—"referent"—that a word represents. The denotation of a word is its core meaning, its dictionary meaning. *Connotation* is the subjective, emotional association that a word has for one person or a group of people. Poets often choose words that contribute to the poem's meaning on both a denotational and a connotational level. You should be alert to such choices.

Questions about diction   You should examine the words in a poem for all their possible shades and levels of meaning. Then you should ask how these meanings combine to create an overall effect. Note the effect that connotation creates in William Wordsworth's "A Slumber Did My Spirit Seal":

A SLUMBER DID MY SPIRIT SEAL

WILLIAM WORDSWORTH

A slumber did my spirit seal;
    I had no human fears—
She seemed a thing that could not feel
    The touch of earthly years.

No motion has she now, no force;
    She neither hears nor sees;
Rolled round in earth's diurnal course,
    With rocks, and stones, and trees.

In order to create the stark contrast between the active, airy girl of the first stanza with the inert, dead girl of the second, Wordsworth relies partly on the connotative effect of the last line. We know the denotative meaning of "rocks and stones and trees," but in this context the emotional or connotative meaning is unpleasant and grating. Rocks and stones are inanimate, cold, cutting, impersonal. And although we usually think of trees as beautiful and majestic, here the association of trees with rocks and stones makes us think of tree roots, of dirt, and thus of the girl's burial. The rocks and stones and trees are not only nonhuman; they confine and smother the girl. Another example of connotation is the word "diurnal," which means "daily." But the Latinate "diurnal" has a slightly more formal connotation than the prosaic "daily." The effect of the word is to make the processes of nature—death, the revolving of the earth, the existence of rocks and stones and trees—seem remote, remorseless, and inevitable.

Imagery—descriptive language

When applied to poetry, the term *imagery* has two meanings. First, imagery represents the descriptive passages of a poem. Although the word "imagery" calls to mind the visual sense, poetic imagery appeals to all the senses. Sensuous imagery is pleasurable for its own sake, but it also provides concreteness and immediacy. Imagery causes the reader to become personally, experientially involved in the subject matter of the poem. Furthermore, the poet often uses descriptive imagery to underscore other elements in a poem. The selection of detail and the vividness imparted to images help create tone, meaning, and characterization.

An example of descriptive imagery is the first stanza of John Keats's narrative poem "The Eve of St. Agnes":

> St. Agnes' Eve—Ah, bitter chill it was!
> The owl, for all his feathers, was a-cold;
> The hare limped trembling through the frozen grass,
> And silent was the flock in woolly fold;
> Numb were the Beadsman's fingers, while he told
> His rosary, and while his frosted breath,
> Like pious incense from a censer old,
> Seemed taking flight for heaven, without a death,
> Past the sweet Virgin's picture, while his prayer he saith.

This stanza appeals to the thermal sense (the chill of the evening, the frozen grass), the sense of touch (the beadsman's numb fingers), the visual sense (the beadsman saying his rosary before the picture of the Virgin), the sense of motion (the hare trembling and limping through the grass, the beadsman's frosted breath taking flight toward heaven), and the sense of sound (the silent flock, the sound of the Beadsman's monotonous prayer). But the dominant sensuous appeal is to the thermal sense. Keats uses every sensuous image in the stanza to make us feel how cold the night is.

Imagery—figurative language

Critics today use *imagery* in a second sense. They use it to mean figurative language, especially metaphor. *Figurative language* is the conscious departure from normal or conventional ways of saying things. This could mean merely a rearrangement of the normal word order of a sentence, such as the following: "Sir Gawain the dragon slew" or "This do in remembrance of me." Such unusual rearrangements are called "rhetorical" figures of speech. But much more common and important to poetry is a second category of figurative language, *tropes*. Tropes (literally, "turns") extend the meaning of words beyond their literal meaning, and the most common form of trope is metaphor. *Metaphor* has both a general and a specific meaning. Generally, it means any analogy (an *analogy* is a partial similarity between two things upon which a comparison may be based). Specifically, metaphor means a particular kind of analogy and is contrasted with the simile. A *simile* is a comparison of two things that are essentially different, and it is signaled by the use of "like" or "as"; for example, "Her tears were like falling rain." The following stanza from Shakespeare's "Fair Is My Love" contains several similes (indicated by the italics):

> Fair is my love, but not so fair as fickle;
> *Mild as a dove*, but neither true nor trusty;
> Brighter than glass, and yet, *as glass is, brittle;*
> Softer than wax, and yet, *as iron, rusty;*
>> A lily pale, with damask dye to grace her;
>> None fairer, nor none falser to deface her.

A metaphor also compares things that are essentially unlike, but it eliminates the comparative words and thus equates the compared items. For example, "My heart was a tornado of passion." The poem "Love Is a Sickness" by Samuel Daniel contains several metaphors (indicated by the italics):

LOVE IS A SICKNESS

SAMUEL DANIEL

> *Love is a sickness* full of woes,
>> All remedies refusing.
> *A plant* that with most cutting grows,
>> Most barren with best using.
>>> Why so?
> More we enjoy it, more it dies,
> If not enjoyed it sighing cries,
>> Hey ho.
>
> *Love is* a torment of the mind,
>> *A tempest* everlasting,
> And Jove hath made it of a kind

> Not well, nor full, nor fasting.
>   Why so?
> More we enjoy it, more it dies,
> If not enjoyed it sighing cries,
>   Hey ho.

Analogies can be directly stated or implied. The similes and metaphors in the above poems by Shakespeare and Daniel are directly stated analogies, but when Daniel in the last lines of each stanza says that love "sighs," he implies a kind of analogy called "personification"; that is, he pretends that love has the attributes of a person. When the poet develops just one analogy throughout the whole poem, the analogy is called an "extended metaphor." Thomas Campion's "There Is a Garden in Her Face" contains an extended metaphor comparing the features of a woman's face to the features of a garden:

THERE IS A GARDEN IN HER FACE

THOMAS CAMPION

> There is a garden in her face,
> Where roses and white lilies grow,
> A heavenly paradise is that place,
> Wherein all pleasant fruits do flow.
> There cherries grow, which none may buy
> Till "Cherry ripe!"° themselves do cry.
>
> Those cherries fairly do enclose
> Of orient pearl a double row;
> Which when her lovely laughter shows,
> They look like rosebuds filled with snow.
> Yet them nor peer nor prince can buy,
> Till "Cherry ripe!" themselves do cry.
>
> Her eyes like angels watch them still;
> Her brows like bended bows do stand,
> Threatening with piercing frowns to kill
> All that attempt with eye or hand
> Those sacred cherries to come nigh,
> Till "Cherry ripe!" themselves do cry.

°A familiar cry of London street vendors

Questions about imagery   Imagery is an important—
some would argue the most important—characteristic of poetry.
You should always identify the imagery of a poem. Ask, then, what
senses the poet appeals to and what analogies he or she implies or
states directly. But you should also ask, *Why* does the poet use
these particular images and analogies? In "Dover Beach," for example, Arnold meaningfully uses both descriptive and metaphorical
imagery. He emphasizes two senses, the visual and the aural. He
begins with the visual—the moon, the lights of France across the
water, the cliffs, the tranquil bay—and throughout the poem he
associates hope and beauty with what the speaker sees. But the poet
soon introduces the aural sense—the grating roar of the sea—
which serves as an antithesis to the visual sense. These two senses
create a tension that mirrors the conflict in the speaker's mind. The
first two stanzas show the speaker merely drifting into a perception
of this conflict, connecting sight with hope and sound with sadness. But by the third stanza, he has become intellectually alert to
the full implications of the conflict. He signals this alertness with a
carefully worked out analogy, his comparison of the sea with faith.
By the fourth stanza, he sums up his despairing conclusion with a
stunning and famous simile:

> And we are here as on a darkling plain
> Swept with confused alarms of struggle and flight,
> Where ignorant armies clash by night.

This final analogy achieves several purposes. First, it brings
the implications of the descriptive imagery to a logical conclusion.
No longer can the speaker draw hope from visual beauty; in this
image, he cannot see at all—it is night, the plain is dark. He can
only hear, but the sound now is more chaotic and directly threatening than the mere ebb and flow of the sea. Second, the analogy
provides an abrupt change of setting. Whereas before the speaker
visualized an unpeopled plain, now he imagines human beings as
agents of destruction. He implies that a world without faith must
seem and be unavoidably arbitrary and violent. Finally, the analogy
allows the speaker to identify his own place in this new world order. Only loyalty is pure and good, so he and his companion must
cling to each other and maneuver through the world's minefields as
best they can.

Rhythm

All human speech has rhythm, but poetry regularizes that rhythm into recognizable patterns. These patterns are called *meters*. Metrical patterns vary depending on the sequence in which one arranges the accented (á) and unaccented (ă) syllables of an utterance. The unit that determines that arrangement is the foot. A *foot* is one unit of rhythm in a verse. Probably the most natural foot in English is the iambic, which has an unaccented syllable followed by an accented syllable (ăá). Here are the most common metrical feet:

iamb (iambic) ăá	ăbóve
trochee (trochaic) áă	lóvelў
anapest (anapestic) ăăá	ŏvĕrwhélm
dactyl (dactylic) áăă	róyăltў
spondee (spondaic) áá	drúmbéat

Poets further determine the arrangement of metrical patterns by the number of feet in each line. The following names apply to the lengths of poetic lines:

monometer (one foot)
dimeter (two feet)
trimeter (three feet)
tetrameter (four feet)
pentameter (five feet)
hexameter (six feet)
heptameter (seven feet)
octameter (eight feet)

A very common line in English poetry is "iambic pentameter"; it contains five iambic feet. Examples of iambic pentameter are the sonnets on page 66–67. Because individuals hear and speak a language in different ways, "scanning" a poem (determining its accented and unaccented syllables and thus its metrical pattern) is not an exact science. But usually poets establish metrical patterns easily and readers detect them equally easily.

Questions about rhythm   Metrics has many uses in poetry. It provides a method of ordering material. It creates a hypnotic effect that rivets attention on the poem. Like the rhythmic qualities of music, it is enjoyable in itself. But probably its greatest importance is that it establishes a pattern from which the poet can depart. By making occasional variations on the pattern, the poet can emphasize specific parts of the poem's content. The sample essay on Emily Dickinson's "Because I could not stop for death" (see Chapter 12) calls attention to such a meaningful variation. The following nursery rhyme offers another example:

> Jáck bĕ/nímblĕ,/Jáck bĕ/ quíck
> Jáck júmp/óvĕr thĕ/cándlĕ/stíck.

The standard metrical pattern in this poem is trochaic tetrameter. The variation comes with "Jáck júmp" (a spondee) followed by "óvĕr thĕ" (a dactyl), both of which emphasize and even represent what Jack does.

Questions to ask about rhythm in poetry, then, are these: What metrical pattern does the poem use? What is appealing about the pattern? Most important, what do the pattern and *departures from it* add to the poem's meaning?

Sound

Poets delight in the sound of language and consciously present sounds to be enjoyed for themselves. They also use them to emphasize meaning, action, and emotion, and especially to call the reader's attention to the relationship of certain words. Rhyme, for example, has the effect of linking words together. Among the most common sound devices are the following:

onomatopaeia—the use of words that sound like what they mean ("buzz," "boom," "hiss," "fizz").

alliteration—the repetition of consonant sounds at the beginning of words or at the beginning of accented syllables ("the *w*oeful *w*oman *w*ent *w*ading *W*ednesday").

assonance—the repetition of vowel sounds followed by different consonant sounds (*O*, the gr*o*ans that *o*pened to his ears").

consonance (or *half-rhyme*)—the repetition of final consonant sounds that are preceded by different vowel sounds (the bea*st* climbed fa*st* to the cre*st*").

rhyme—the repetition of accented vowels and the sounds that follow. There are subcategories of "rhyme":

> *masculine rhyme* (the rhymed sounds have only one syllable: "m*an*-r*an*," "det*ect*-corr*ect*").

> *feminine rhyme* (the rhymed sounds have two or more syllables: "*subtle*-re*buttal*,"
> "de*ceptively*-per*ceptively*").

> *internal rhyme* (the rhymed sounds are within the line).

> *end rhyme* (the rhymed sounds appear at the ends of lines).

> *approximate rhyme* (the words are close to rhyming: "book-buck," "watch-match," "man-in").

Edgar Allan Poe's "To Helen" illustrates many of these sound devices:

TO HELEN

EDGAR ALLAN POE

Helen, thy beauty is to me
Like those Nicean barks of yore,
That gently, o'er a perfumed sea,
The weary, way-worn wanderer bore
To his own native shore.

On desperate seas long wont to roam
Thy hyacinth hair, thy classic face
Thy Naiad airs have brought me home
To the glory that was Greece
And the grandeur that was Rome.

Lo! in yon brilliant window-nich
How statue-like I see thee stand!
The agate lamp within thy hand,
Ah! Psyche, from the regions which
Are Holy Land!

masculine rhyme/ end rhyme

alliteration

consonance

approximate rhyme

assonance

internal rhyme

Questions about sound   It's easy to lose yourself in an analysis of the mechanical intricacies of a poem's sound structure and forget why you are making the analysis in the first place. You want to ask, What sound devices does the poet use? But you also want to ask, Why does the poet use them? How do they help establish the poem's tone, atmosphere, theme, setting, characterization, and emotional qualities? In Poe's "To Helen," for example, the alliteration in the fourth line ("*w*eary, *w*ay-*w*orn *w*anderer") underscores the fatigued state of the wanderer. The consonance of "seas" and "airs" in lines 6 and 8 emphasizes the contrast between them; one is "desperate" but the other assuages despair. And the assonance in line 11 ("*i*n yon br*i*lliant w*i*ndow-n*i*ch"), with its emphasis on high, tight, "i" sounds, helps to characterize the luminousness of the place where Helen, statuelike, stands.

Structure

Poets give structure to their poems in two overlapping ways: by organizing ideas according to a logical plan and by creating a pattern of sounds. Arnold arranges "Dover Beach" in both ways, as do most poets. He divides the poem into four units, each of which has a pattern of end rhyme, and he arranges the whole poem rhetorically—that is, by ideas. Each unit elaborates a single point, and each point follows logically from the preceding one.

Perhaps the most common sound device by which poets create structure is end rhyme, and any pattern of end rhyme is called a *rhyme scheme*. Rhyme scheme helps to establish another structural device, the *stanza,* which is physically separated from other stanzas by extra spaces and usually represents one idea. Poets, of course, can create any rhyme scheme or stanza form they choose, but they often work instead within the confines of already established poetic structures. These are called *fixed forms*. The most famous fixed form in English is the *sonnet*. Like other fixed forms, the sonnet provides ready-made structural divisions by which a poet can organize ideas. But it also challenges poets to mold unwieldy material into an unyielding structure. The result is a tension between material and form that is pleasing both to poet and reader.

All sonnets have fourteen lines of iambic pentameter. There are two kinds of sonnets, both named for their most famous practitioners. A *Shakespearean sonnet* rhymes abab/cdcd/efef/gg and has a structural division of three quatrains (that is, each containing four lines) and a couplet. A *Petrarchan sonnet* rhymes abbaabba/cdecde and contains an octave (eight lines) followed by a sestet (six lines). Alternate rhyme schemes for the sestet are cdcdcd and cdedce. The following poems illustrate each kind of sonnet:

SONNET 116

WILLIAM SHAKESPEARE

Let me not to the marriage of true minds	a	
Admit impediments. Love is not love	b	
Which alters when it alteration finds,	a	
Or bends with the remover to remove:	b	4
Oh, no! it is an ever-fixèd mark,	c	
That looks on tempests and is never shaken;	d	
It is the star to every wandering bark,	c	
Whose worth's unknown, although his height be taken,	d	8
Love's not Time's fool, though rosey lips and cheeks	e	
Within his bending sickle's compass come;	f	
Love alters not with his brief hours and weeks,	e	
But bears it out even to the edge of doom.	f	12
If this be error and upon me proved,	g	
I never writ, nor no man ever loved.	g	14

quatrains applies to the first twelve lines; *couplet* applies to the final two lines.

Shakespeare molds the ideas and images of this poem to fit its form perfectly. He states the theme—that love remains constant no matter what—in the first quatrain. In the second, he says that cataclysmic events cannot destroy love. In the third, he says that time cannot destroy love. Finally, in the couplet, he affirms the truth of his theme.

THE WORLD IS TOO MUCH WITH US

WILLIAM WORDSWORTH

The world is too much with us; late and soon,	a	
Getting and spending, we lay waste our powers;	b	
Little we see in nature that is ours;	b	
We have given our hearts away, a sordid boon!	a	4
This Sea that bares her bosom to the moon,	a	
The winds that will be howling at all hours,	b	
And are up-gathered now like sleeping flowers,	b	
For this, for everything, we are out of tune;	a	8

octave applies to the first eight lines.

	It moves us not. —Great God! I'd rather be	c
sestet	A Pagan suckled in a creed outworn;	d
	So might I, standing on this pleasant lea,	c
	Have glimpses that would make me less forlorn;	d
	Have sight of Proteus rising from the sea;	c
	Or hear old Triton blow his wreathèd horn.	d 14

Wordsworth uses the structure of the Petrarchan sonnet to shape his ideas. In the octave he states his general theme—that materialistic values and activities dull our sensitivity to nature. But he divides the octave into two quatrains. In the first he states his theme; in the second he exemplifies it. He then uses the sestet to suggest an alternate attitude, one that might produce a greater appreciation of nature's mystery and majesty.

Questions about structure   You can find definitions of many fixed forms by looking them up in handbooks of literature (see the bibliography at the end of this chapter)—the ballad, the ode, the heroic couplet, the Alexandrine stanza, the rhyme royal stanza, the Spenserian stanza, and so forth. But since poets do not always use fixed forms, and since there are many ways to give poetry structure, you should try to answer this question: What devices does the poet use to give the poem structure? Does the poet use rhyme scheme, stanzas, double spaces, indentations, repetition of words and images, line lengths, rhetorical organization? But as with rhythm and sound, a follow-up question is of equal consequence: How does the poem's structure emphasize or relate to its meaning? An example of such a relationship is the final stanza of "Dover Beach," in which Arnold uses end rhyme to emphasize opposing world views:

Ah, love, let us be true	a
To one another! for the world, which seems	b
To lie before us like a land of dreams,	b
So various, so beautiful, so new,	a
Hath really neither joy, nor love, nor light,	c
Nor certitude, nor peace, nor help for pain;	d
And we are here as on a darkling plain	d
Swept with confused alarms of struggle and flight,	c
Where ignorant armies clash by night.	c

The rhyme scheme of the first four lines is almost the same as the next five lines; the only difference is the addition of the fifth line. This similarity divides the stanza in half, and the difference in rhymes corresponds to the difference of the ideas in the two halves.

FOR FURTHER STUDY

Drama

Bentley, Eric. *The Life of the Drama*. New York: Atheneum, 1964.

Esslin, Martin. *An Anatomy of Drama*. New York: Hill and Wang, 1976.

Whiting, Frank M. *An Introduction to the Theatre*. 4th ed. New York: Harper & Row, 1978.

The books by Eric Bentley and Martin Esslin are thorough treatments of drama by well-known drama critics; both books include explanations of comedy and tragedy. The book by Whiting discusses not just drama but "theater," the production of plays.

Poetry

Boulton, Marjorie. *The Anatomy of Poetry*. London: Routledge and Kegan Paul, 1953.

Fussel, Paul, Jr. *Poetic Meter and Poetic Form*. New York: Random House, 1967.

Holman, C. Hugh. *A Handbook to Literature*. 4th ed. Indianapolis, Ind.: Odyssey, 1980.

MacLeish, Archibald. *Poetry and Experience*. Boston: Houghton Mifflin, 1961.

Reeves, James. *Understanding Poetry*. New York: Barnes and Noble, 1965.

Marjorie Boulton's *The Anatomy of Poetry* and James Reeves' *Understanding Poetry* offer thorough explanations of the elements of poetry. Both attempt the difficult task of defining "poetry." Paul

Fussell, Jr., provides a lucid explanation of metrical patterns and poetic structures and how one uses them to analyze poetry. His book concludes with an inviting bibliography. Archibald MacLeish is a fine American poet who, in *Poetry and Experience,* offers his own view of poetry. Hugh Holman's *Handbook to Literature* is an encyclopedia of literary terms.

5

How to generate topics by using specialized approaches

I N CHAPTERS 3 AND 4 we described an approach to analyzing literature that utilizes only the facts provided in the works themselves. Other approaches, however, often require specialized knowledge, knowledge of disciplines other than literature. Although some of these approaches are so specialized that only graduate students or full-time scholars would use them, many are accessible to any serious student and are good sources of essay topics. This chapter describes five of them.

HISTORICAL CRITICISM

Historical criticism is a method of studying literature by period and movement. This approach recognizes that literary phenomena—methods of composition, subject matter, and philosophical outlook—characterize various historical periods. Thus, the use of blank verse in plays characterizes the Shakespearean era; the use of heroic couplets the Neoclassical era. An emphasis on free will characterizes the Romantic movement; a philosophy of determinism the Realistic and Naturalistic movements. A focus on hedonistic self-indulgence distinguishes the 1920s; a focus on social conflict the 1930s. The historical approach also assumes that literary periods and movements are dynamic. As one period reaches exhaustion, another period begins.

The historical approach has several goals: to study a work's relationship to its own and other periods, to learn more about a writer's culture, to place the work within an evolving tradition (like the novel, Christian literature, allegory, political fiction, the epic), to compare it with the literature of other countries. But the most important goal of historical criticism is to illuminate the work. We know, for example, that Jack London read the most influential thinkers of his day, Darwin and Spencer; by studying their ideas, we understand better the philosophical implications of London's fiction. T. S. Eliot, like other poets of the early twentieth century, studied the French Symbolist poets; by studying their poetry, we understand Eliot's methods better. John Steinbeck depicted the social dislocations of poor people in the 1930s, and by studying their problems and the social theories prominent then, we understand his themes better.

Undergraduate survey courses typically use a historical approach. They present a country's literature chronologically or thematically and show how authors exemplify their periods. The papers you write for survey courses will often focus on the relationship between a work and its historical context. One way to generate paper topics for these courses is to apply definitions of social, intellectual, and literary trends to individual works—definitions of concepts like Romanticism, Realism, Neoclassicism, Symbolism, Renaissance, Modernism, Surrealism, Darwinism, Imagism, Naturalism. The most obvious source of these definitions is your instructor, but you can also find good definitions in dictionaries of literary terms, literary histories, encyclopedias, history books, and other sources of background information. Another source of essay topics is comparisons—comparisons of works from different movements, comparisons of works from the same period. A third source is the cultural traits authors describe or draw upon for their themes. William Faulkner, for example, used the "Southern Myth" in his fiction—a nostalgic, glorified concept of Southern ideals and history that evolved before the Civil War and received acute enlargement afterward. Faulkner never says directly that he focuses on this myth, but by studying Southern history and observing the myth in other works, we can see that he does so, and thus we can understand better the unspoken, implied tensions in his work.

Two standard (and massive) examples of historical criticism are Robert E. Spiller et al., eds., *The Literary History of the United States,* 4th ed. rev. (New York: Macmillan, 1974) and Albert C. Baugh et al., eds., *The Literary History of England,* 2nd ed. (New York: Appleton-Century-Crofts, 1967). A book that develops a thesis about the relationship between history and literature is Robert E. Spiller's *The Cycle of American Literature: An Essay in Historical Criticism* (New York: The Free Press, 1967). A fine historical treatment of a genre is Walter Allen's *The English Novel: A Short Critical History* (New York: Dutton, 1954).

BIOGRAPHICAL CRITICISM

The biographical approach relates the author's life and thought to his or her works. Usually the author's life and thought are reflections of his or her time and are thus important aspects of the historical approach. Sometimes a writer may have been ahead of his or her time, even unclassifiable. Or the writer may have been the predominant figure of the time. Or the writer's life may have been the major source of his or her literary material. For whatever reason, a writer's life may shed light on his or her literature and the literature of the era.

The biographical approach has two major advantages. First, it helps to illuminate elements within a work—words, allusions to local and historical events, conflicts, themes, characters, setting. Learning, for example, that F. Scott Fitzgerald had an ambivalent attitude toward people with great wealth prompts us to look for a similar ambivalence in his works. Second, works often take on an added significance when we see them as expressions of authors' deep concerns and conflicts. The more we empathize with a writer's problems, the more meaningful his or her works may seem to us. The more we know about the full historical and biographical context of a work's themes, the more relevant they may seem to all human experience.

If you use the biographical approach, avoid two mistakes. First, avoid equating the work's contents with the author's life.

They are never the same. No matter what the source of a work's material may be, it is a recreation of life, a stylization and alteration of it. Literature is "fictional." Some scholars argue that this is even true of "nonfictional" writings like memoirs and autobiographies. Second, avoid using unsound sources of information. Many biographies are highly speculative or contain erroneous information. Not until the twentieth century, for example, did we have a biography of Edgar Allan Poe that did not distort, sometimes grossly, the facts about his life.

Three very fine and enjoyable examples of biographical criticism are K. J. Fielding's *Charles Dickens: A Critical Introduction* (Boston: Houghton Mifflin, 1964), F. W. Dupee's *Henry James: His Life and Writings* (Garden City, N.Y.: Doubleday, 1956), and Arthur Mizener's *The Far Side of Paradise: A Biography of F. Scott Fitzgerald* (Houghton Mifflin, 1965).

SOCIAL CRITICISM

You may want to investigate and use three other, much more specialized approches to examining literature: social criticism, psychological criticism, and archetypal criticism. Social criticism is similar to historical criticism in recognizing literature as a reflection of its environment. It would focus, for example, on the ways in which Jane Austen's novels depict the emphasis on decorum and etiquette by the English country gentry around the turn of the nineteenth century. But in recent times, social criticism has described a particular kind of social reality and sometimes a particular economic and social theory. Social critics were most active in the 1930s during the Great Depression. They applauded literature that depicted the struggles of the poor and downtrodden, especially when they engaged in strikes against oppressive capitalist bosses. Examples of literature with such strong "proletarian" elements are the works of Carl Sandburg, Émile Zola, Maxim Gorky, Nicolai Gogol, Frank Norris, Charles Dickens, Richard Wright, John Steinbeck, Theodore Dreiser, John Dos Passos, and James T. Farrell. The social critics usually approved of a socialist solution to the problems of the oppressed, and they sometimes judged the quality of works solely on the basis of their Marxist orientation. Partly because of this narrowness of focus and rigidity of standards, the social approach has lost some of its appeal since the 1930s. It showed, however, that many works do reflect society in great detail, that they sometimes attempt to reform society, and that understanding them means in part grappling with the social issues they reflect. A well-known and thoroughgoing work of social criticism is Granville Hicks's *The Great Tradition: An Interpretation of American Literature Since the Civil War* (New York: Macmillan, 1935).

If the social approach seems relevant to the work you want to write about, you should first define the social situation the work describes and identify the author's attitude toward it. Does the author, for example, seem to have solutions in mind? Does he or she feel that society has to be the way he or she describes it? If you suspect that the author depicts a historical situation and you want to compare his or her treatment with the actual events, then you will need to seek out reliable secondary sources. And if you want to argue that particular economic or social theories help to explain the author's social concerns in a work, you will need reliable explanations of those theories.

PSYCHOLOGICAL CRITICISM

A second highly specialized approach is psychological criticism, which attempts to apply modern psychological theories to authors and their works. Because of the predominance of Freudian psychology in the twentieth century, psychological criticism usually relies upon the theories of Sigmund Freud. Freud's ideas are complex and multiple; not all of them relate to literature. But literary critics find three of them very attractive: the dominance of the unconscious mind over the conscious, the expression of the unconscious mind through symbols (most notably in dreams), and the primacy of sexuality as a motivating force in human behavior. These three ideas are related. Freud believed that sexual drives reside in the unconscious, that the conscious mind represses them, and that unconscious symbols usually represent this repressed sexual energy.

Freudian critics see literature as a kind of "dream" and thus a source of insight into the authors themselves. This area of psychological criticism is biographical rather than literary criticism. But psychological critics also look on characters as having motivations, conflicts, desires, and inclinations similar to those of real people. And these critics look for psychological clues to the makeup of literary characters, especially the unconscious symbolic expressions found in dreams and repeated patterns of behavior and speech. In Eugene O'Neill's *Long Day's Journey into Night,* for example, whenever Mary Tyrone raises her hands to her hair, she unconsciously expresses anxiety about her wrecked youth, health, and innocence. Many authors purposely incorporate psychological theories in their works. Eugene O'Neill, D. H. Lawrence, Sherwood Anderson, and Tennessee Williams, for example, were familiar with Freudian psychology. Some writers employ structural devices drawn from psychological theories. Examples are the "stream of consciousness" technique, which conforms to William James's ideas about the workings of the conscious mind, and the surrealistic technique, which conforms to Freud's ideas about the undisciplined unconscious. Examples of stream-of-consciousness narration are James Joyce's *Portrait of the Artist as a Young Man* and *Ulysses,* William Faulkner's *The Sound and the Fury,* T. S. Eliot's "The Love Song of J. Alfred Prufrock," Virginia Woolf's *To the Lighthouse,* and O'Neill's *Strange Interlude.* Examples of surrealism are Joyce's *Finnegans Wake* and the fiction of Franz Kafka.

Many other works of literature are also rich fields for psychological criticism, even though they may not have been directly influenced by psychological theories. Freudian critics are interested in any works that are themselves dreamlike, such as Lewis Carroll's *Alice in Wonderland,* or that contain accounts of characters' dreams, as do some of Dostoevsky's novels. Other works appeal to psychological critics because of their heavy emphasis on complex or unusual characters.

One of the most influential works of psychological criticism is Ernest Jones's *Hamlet and Oedipus* (New York: Norton, 1949), in which Jones, a psychiatrist, argues that Hamlet's problems stem from Oedipal conflicts. An anthology of psychological criticism is Hendrik M. Ruitenbeck, ed., *Psychoanalysis and Literature* (New York: Dutton, 1964).

If you apply the psychological approach to works of literature, make sure that you have a good source of information about the theories you use. Avoid applying psychological theories rigidly. Make sure that evidence in the works supports your use of them.

ARCHETYPAL CRITICISM

The third of these more specialized approaches is the archetypal. Archetypal criticism emerged from the theories of the Swiss psychologist Carl Jung. Jung accepted Freud's concept of the unconscious mind, but whereas Freud held that each person's unconscious is unique, Jung argued that a part of the unconscious is linked by historical associations and communal "memories" to the unconscious minds of all people. To represent this phenomenon, he coined the phrase "collective unconscious." He believed that certain human products and activities—myth, symbols, ritual, literature—reproduced these memories in the form of "archetypes." Jung defined an *archetype* as any figure or pattern that recurred in works of the imagination from generation to generation.

Archetypal characters

Although there are many possible archetypes, they fall into three broad categories. The first, characters, contains such figures as the hero, the rake, the scapegoat, the outcast, the hypersensitive youth, the earth mother, the martyr, the *femme fatale,* the rebel, the cruel stepmother, the saint, the "spiritual" woman, the tyrannical father, star-crossed lovers, the ruler. The following are examples of literary treatments of some of these archetypes: the *femme fatale* (Shakespeare's *Antony and Cleopatra,* Prosper Mérimee's *Carmen,* Keats's "La Belle Dame Sans Merci," Zola's *Nana*); the tyrannical father (Rudolph Besier's *The Barretts of Wimpole Street,* Shakespeare's *King Lear,* Longfellow's *Hiawatha*); the hero (Hemingway's *For Whom the Bell Tolls,* Cooper's *The Last of the Mohicans,* Malory's *Morte d'Arthur,* the anonymous *Sir Gawain and the Green Knight,* Homer's *The Iliad*); the scapegoat (Shirley Jackson's "The Lottery," Melville's *Billy Budd*); the outcast (Dickens' *Great Expectations,* Victor Hugo's *The Hunchback of Notre Dame,* the Book of Job, Coleridge's "The Rime of the Ancient Mariner," Tennyson's "The Lady of Shalott"); the rake (Byron's *Don Juan,* Samuel Richardson's *Clarissa,* Etheridge's *The Man of Mode,* Goldsmith's *She Stoops to Conquer,* Marvell's "To His Coy Mistress," Wycherley's *The Country Wife*);

and star-crossed lovers (Marlowe's "Hero and Leander," Shakespeare's *Romeo and Juliet*, Hawthorne's *The Scarlet Letter*).

Archetypal situations

The second category, situations, includes the quest, the initiation, the journey, the fall, death and rebirth, and the task. Some works, like *Oedipus Rex*, contain more than one archetypal situation. Oedipus makes a "quest" for the truth about King Laius' murderer. He has already performed a task—answering the Sphinx's question—that saved the kingdom. And when he achieves his quest, he suffers a catastrophic fall (from highest in the land to lowest). The quest is usually combined with a journey, as in the search for the Holy Grail of Arthurian legend, and often results in the initiation of a naïve, inexperienced protagonist into the hardship and complexity of life. Examples of works dealing with initiation are Hawthorne's "Young Goodman Brown," Joyce's "Araby," Dickens' *Great Expectations*, Fitzgerald's *The Great Gatsby*, Crane's *The Red Badge of Courage*, and Hardy's *Jude the Obscure*. The death-rebirth archetype appears in myth and fantasy as the literal death and rebirth of a character—Snow White and Sleeping Beauty, for example—but in more realistic literature it often appears in connection with seasonal changes: fall (old age), winter (death), spring (rebirth), summer (life and fruition). In such works, seasonal changes emphasize the metaphorical death and rebirth of a character or place. For example, Émile Zola's *Germinal* concludes with spring, and the renewal of plant and animal life coincides with the end of the workers' strike. The mining town has "died" as an economic entity, but with the end of the strike it is reborn. Spring also represents the germination and growth of ideas that will lead to a better life for the workers. Often allied with the death-rebirth situation is a descent into hell. In some works, like Homer's *The Odyssey*, Virgil's *The Aeneid*, and Dante's *The Divine Comedy*, the protagonist literally descends to hell. But in works that shun fantasy, the journey is metaphorical and equivalent to a traversal of hell-like places (T. S. Eliot's *The Waste Land*) or to psychological states of deep despair. Dostoevsky's Raskolnikov in *Crime and Punishment* emerges at the end from a psychological hell brought on by his cold-blooded murder of an innocent person. Tennessee Williams' play *Orpheus Descending* and Jean Cocteau's film "Orphé" are conscious metaphorical uses of the journey-into-hell archetype.

Archetypal symbols and associations

The third category of archetypes is symbols and associations, many of which suggest polarities. Examples are light-darkness (light equals knowledge, hope, purity, spirituality; dark equals ignorance, despair, evil, bestiality), water-desert (water equals rebirth, life, creativity; desert equals spiritual and intellectual sterility, death), heights-depths (heights equal achievement, sublimity, heaven, revelation, purity; depths equal dejection, mystery, entrapment, hell, death), and the already mentioned spring-winter. One critic argues that Hemingway's novels utilize the height-depth polarity: when Hemingway's characters occupy high places, things go well for them; when they descend to the lowlands, the fragile order of their world falls apart.

The appeal of archetypal criticism

Jung's theories are controversial among psychologists, but they have attracted literary critics for several reasons. One is that remarkably similar patterns do exist from culture to culture. Early Christian missionaries, for example, encountered myths celebrating a martyred, resurrected hero who promised to return and bring a new, golden age. Such was the case when the Aztecs mistook Cortez for the god Quetzalcoatl. Another reason is Jung's contention that archetypes have a profound emotional and intellectual impact on people, that people unconsciously recognize them as being somehow profoundly meaningful. This theory helps critics to explain, apart from aesthetics, the long-lasting appeal of such works as *Oedipus Rex,* the *Odyssey,* portions of the Bible, the Greek myths, and fairy tales. And the archetypal approach helps to explain the appeal of art forms that lack high aesthetic quality but that are nonetheless very popular, like American westerns, detective and spy stories, and soap operas. In fact, critics often use the archetypal approach to understand not just the literature of a culture but the culture itself. A culture's recurring emphasis on extensive travel, for example, might suggest restlessness and rootlessness. Or patterns featuring strong, dominant females might suggest a diminished masculine role. Or recurrent violence might indicate a lack of patience to solve complex problems peacefully and lastingly. Archetypal critics have made all of these points about American society.

Perhaps the most practical attraction of archetypal criticism is simply the recognition that patterns in literature do exist and recur, that they often give structure to a work, that many artists have employed them in one way or another, and that, for whatever reason, they often deal with profound aspects of human experience. You don't have to believe in Jung's theories to use the archetypal approach to literature. You need only be alert to the possibility of recurring patterns and write about them if you find them meaningful.

A work that deals provocatively with one archetype is Joseph Campbell's *The Hero with a Thousand Faces* (New York: Pantheon Books, 1949). Two controversial but enjoyable works of archetypal literary criticism by Leslie A. Fiedler are *Love and Death in the American Novel*, rev. ed. (New York: Stein and Day, 1966) and *No! in Thunder: Essays on Myth and Literature* (New York: Stein and Day, 1972). The most important spokesman for archetypal criticism is Northrop Frye. See especially his *The Educated Imagination* (Bloomington: Indiana University Press, 1964) and *Anatomy of Criticism* (Princeton, N. J.: Princeton Univ. Press, 1957). A work that wonderfully spoofs all the critical approaches to literature is Frederick C. Crews's *The Pooh Perplex* (New York: Dutton, 1965).

6

How to generate topics by evaluating the quality of literature

EVALUATING THE QUALITY of works is basic to all serious reading of literature. Teachers who create literature courses on whatever level of sophistication choose works because they are "good," and individual readers decide whether works are good "for them." It is perhaps inevitable that we rate what we read even on the most superficial level: "Boy, I really enjoyed that play"; "That book was really boring." In addition to appraising the quality of works you read, you might also want to write essays about their strengths and weaknesses. This chapter provides some criteria and questions to help you in doing so.

Perhaps the best place to begin is with yourself. Your subjective responses to a work may not be systematic or even logical, but they should help you to begin a systematic and logical analysis of the work's successes and failures. The subjective responses of other readers may be useful too.

1. If you like the work, why do you? Is it the characters, the setting, the mood, the humor, the ideas, the action, the sentiment, the language? Why does it succeed?

2. Does the work move you emotionally? Do you care about its ideas, characters, events? If so, why?

3. If you dislike the work, where specifically does it fail for you? Even if you think highly of a work, what do you perceive to be its flaws?

4. If your acquaintances like or dislike the work, do you agree with their reasons?

Literary critics of all ages have developed their own methods of evaluating literature. They don't always agree, and their standards of excellence vary from age to age and person to person. Their ideas do, however, provide some practical guidelines for judging specific works. In this chapter we will consider some questions that most critics would ask when evaluating works of literature.

IS THE WORK UNIFIED AND COHERENT?

Many critics claim that unity and coherence are a work's most important aesthetic qualities. If a work is unified and coherent, it is "good." If not, it is "bad." A unified work creates a single effect, has a single aim or purpose; a coherent work uses all its elements to attain that effect, to contribute to that aim or purpose.

Modern critics find fault with works containing elements that seem superfluous to an overall purpose. A good example is Sir Walter Scott's novel *Ivanhoe,* which begins with a heavy emphasis on Ivanhoe's relationship with the Saxon heroine Rowena, as if it and she are to be important parts of the novel, and then inexplicably drops them to concentrate on Ivanhoe's troubled relationship with the more exotic and more interesting Rebecca. Also in *Ivanhoe,* one character "dies" in battle, is mourned at length, and then suddenly sits up and proclaims himself recovered. Scott gives no reason for this remarkable reversal; he just puts it in. In fact, Scott often seems to be writing to please the momentary interests of his readers. He wants to tell a good story, not to create unified works of art. Consequently, modern critics downgrade the quality of *Ivanhoe.* They admit that it is a good "read" the first time through, but conclude that it does not reward more careful attention. O. Henry is another writer whom critics deride, in this case for his contrived endings. In his short stories he creates one set of circumstances only to produce endings that don't logically follow from these circumstances. These endings may pleasantly surprise us by their happy turn of events, but they are inconsistent with what precedes them and thus are ultimately unsatisfying.

It may be that modern critics sometimes overemphasize the importance of unity and coherence in literature. Some forms of literature, like novels, long narrative poems, and plays, lend themselves to disparateness. Shakespeare and Dickens include extraneous elements in their works, and yet their works are unquestionably "great." Works that benefit most from the demand for unity and coherence are short works, like stories and poems, in which every word should count toward a total effect and in which coherence is recognizable almost at a glance. But all good works, including long ones, emerge with an *overall* sense of consistency and order, even if a few elements may not seem to fit the pattern. Careful study should reveal such patterns, and continued study should reveal them even more fully.

DOES THE WORK GIVE CONTINUAL PLEASURE?

Does the work give pleasure the first time through? Does it give pleasure on subsequent readings? Answers to these questions are obviously subjective and vary from person to person. One way to answer them is to examine a work's history. If a work has survived several generations of readers, then the answer to both questions might be "yes." If a work was very popular with one generation but with no others, then the answer to the first question might be "yes" and to the second "no." But such historical evidence is inadequate. A work might be rediscovered, or it might never have been popular but nonetheless have been read and reread by an elite group. Or it might be too new to have become popular.

The pleasure-giving quality of literature is mysterious. Two criteria for evaluating it may be helpful. First, some critics hold that novelty and surprise are major causes of pleasure. Thus many novels give pleasure by utilizing exotic settings, unusual characters, and suspenseful plots. Publishers call such novels "page turners" because they compel the reader to keep turning the page to find out what will happen next. The novels of Robert Louis Stevenson, Jack

London, James Fenimore Cooper, Alexander Dumas, Rafael Sabatini, James Michener, Raymond Chandler, Leon Uris, Herman Wouk, Allen Drury, Victoria Holt, and a host of other best-selling writers are examples of page turners. The novelty of the material makes our first-time experience with the work exciting and fun. But good works of art should give pleasure beyond a first-time reading. You should be able to reread them and *continue* to find novelty and be surprised. The limitation of a suspenseful plot is that once you know "what happens," its chief interest is dissipated. If a work continues to be new to you, then it is "good."

A second criterion for evaluating the pleasure a work provides is the distinction critics make between easy and difficult beauty. Difficult beauty, they maintain, is preferable to easy beauty. Elements that give immediate pleasure, like dramatic plots, simple ideas, heroic characters, euphonious language, glamorous settings, and happy endings do not give as lasting satisfaction as materials that seem at first to discourage enjoyment, like tragic events, plain and troubled characters, dissonant language, threatening landscapes, undramatic happenings, pessimistic ideas. The reason may be that the difficult materials emerge from aspects of life that deeply affect us emotionally and intellectually, and we take longer-lasting satisfaction in seeing them put in order, which works of art always do. The easy materials, in other words, give superficial pleasure; the difficult materials give profound pleasure.

IS THE WORK TRUE?

Critics are divided about the importance of "truth" in literature. Some contend that even though a work may represent great ideas, it still may not be good. Others argue that a work can be very skillfully assembled, but if it has no relation to the real world, then it is less good than works that do. Each reader must resolve this controversy to his or her own satisfaction. Probably, however, the works that people read again and again are those that offer some insight into the nature of the real world. In this section we will discuss some questions that should help you to determine the quality of the "truth" offered in literary works.

Is the work meaningful?

Although it is possible to have meaningless works in other media—dance, music, painting, sculpture—it is probably impossible to create a totally meaningless work of literature. The reason is that literature uses an inherently meaningful medium—language. Words are symbols. They connect with aspects of reality, and the stringing of words together into phrases makes them coherent. Words become ideas. Also, literature represents real life, at least superficially, or else we could not understand it. If it did not, it would be another art form, either visual (a kind of "painting") or aural (a kind of "music"), but not literature.

Given this referential level of meaning, however, literature can avoid meaning by creating imaginary worlds that have little practical relation to the real world. Usually this literature is "escapist" because it emphasizes the ideal—characters, settings, and events that rarely exist in the real world. In the dissolute court of Charles II (king of England, 1660–1685), the most popular works of literature were long French romances depicting impossibly honorable courtiers, impossibly beautiful and chaste heroines, all interacting in an impossibly just court. A modern example is Ian Fleming's James Bond thrillers, whose protagonist possesses incredible skills and tolerances, meets an endless sequence of willing, shapely females, gets caught up in bizarre conspiracies (like voodoo on the Southern Railroad), and clashes with supervillains who gain immense power and yet who stupidly tell Bond all their secrets. Usually such works are enjoyable for a single reading, or they are important for what they reflect of the values and tastes of their reading public. But because they have little relation to the real world, they are quickly forgotten. They are not "good" literature.

Does your perception of the real world square with the author's?

One way to assess the meaningfulness of a work is to compare its presentation and interpretation of reality with your own perceptions and experience. Of course, your experience is not the totality of experience. You will want to consider other readers' experiences and reactions to the work. But we are all limited by time and space.

We must base decisions about truth on what we know now, not on what other people know or on what we will know later. Such decisions are still valid and important.

Does the work present the probable and the typical?

Since an author best communicates his or her interpretation of reality by presenting the probable and typical, your assessment of his or her ability to do so is crucial to determining a work's meaningfulness. Examples of atypical characters are the flat characters of melodrama: the unmotivated villain, the pure-as-the-driven-snow heroine, the square-jawed hero. Examples of improbable events are the hero's arrival just in time to rescue the heroine from being sawed in half or run over by a train, the corrupt politician's sudden conversion to righteousness, the imprudent father's avoidance of financial ruin by inheriting a fortune or winning the state lottery.

Does the work present a mature vision of reality?

Any work can offer an interpretation of reality, but some interpretations are immature and simpleminded. More valuable are those that reflect qualities that serious, thoughtful people would recognize. These include a recognition of the world's potential for injustice and tragedy, of the ambiguity inherent in moral choices and judgments, of the complexity of human events and decisions, of the three-dimensionality of human nature. The world is filled, for example, with people who do both evil and good. A mature view recognizes that such people are equal to more than just a limited set of actions. The death-row murderer has some admirable (or at least sympathetic) traits. The philanthropist is capable of destructive acts and of cruelty. All people are flawed and all people have redeeming traits.

Does the work's interpretation of reality deserve serious reflection?

Sometimes we may find ourselves in disagreement with a work's world view. Sinclair Lewis's *Babbitt*, James Joyce's *Ulysses*, Arthur Miller's *The Crucible*, Allen Ginsberg's *Howl*, and D. H. Lawrence's

Lady Chatterley's Lover present views of the world that have been extremely controversial and that many people still find objectionable. If you object to a work's ideas, you can test their quality by asking if the author has rendered them vividly, has represented his or her position fairly (that is, has kept opposing positions in sight), and has focused on ideas that are worth thinking about. One value of literature is that it compels us, through the force and logic of its imagined worlds, to give serious consideration to important concepts with which we are unfamiliar or with which we disagree. If the artist renders his or her ideas compellingly and if they are important, then that is all he or she can be expected to do. The author's ideas are "good." But our recognition of the artistic integrity of a work's ideas does not necessarily mean that we accept their "truth." We may still disagree with them.

Is the work universal?

Does the work transcend the ideology of the author? Does it transcend the narrow concerns, obsessions, and prejudices of one reader, one group, one society, one nation, one generation, one century?

These questions represent the ultimate test of any work of literature. The better a work can "live" beyond the interests of a few readers, the better the work. This doesn't mean that everyone will like the works of Chaucer, Dante, Shakespeare, Spenser, Milton, Wordsworth, Racine, Goethe, Molière, Emily Brontë, Homer, Ovid, Dickens, Emily Dickinson, George Eliot. It means that their works have touched an ever-increasing number of people, that they have universal appeal. It also means that the *ideas* represented in their works are congruent with most people's perception of reality, even though those ideas might emerge from narrow ideological concerns. John Bunyan, for example, was a radical, nonconformist English minister living in a time famous for its fierce religious factionalism. He was a mentally wracked, obsessive Calvinist whose narrative *The Pilgrim's Progress* reflects anguish over his immediate condition—he was in jail—and over his state of grace. He meant it as a guide for members of his own sect. And yet even though its protagonist, "Christian," must travel the straight and narrow Puritan road to the "Celestial City," somehow Christian becomes more than a seventeenth-century Puritan. His struggles, temptations, emotions, and interests are those that we all feel as we make our way through life. His companions may have allegorical names—Obstinate, Hopeful, Faithful, Pliable, Mr. Worldly Wiseman, Talkative, Giant Despair—but they embody people that any of us might meet. His places—Vanity Fair, the Slough of Despond, Doubting Castle, the Valley of the Shadow of Death—have a psychological and even a physical reality that has meaning for all readers. The basic theme of the book—that life threatens and tests our emotional and moral integrity with ambiguous situations—is one that we all recognize as true. Christian could as well be called "Everyman," for his pilgrimage is real to all people, no matter of what faith, nationality, or century.

Are the work's ideas consistent with one another and with the work's form?

A work's ideas must emerge convincingly from its form, not be imposed on that form. One should be able to induce the work's ideas from its materials. No one, including the author, should have to tell us what a work means. Furthermore, if all the elements of a work are logically related to one another and to an overriding purpose, then the work's ideas will also be consistent with one another. A work should not, for example, show us that one thing is true in one part and that a contradictory thing is true in another part. Henry David Thoreau seems to do this in *Walden,* where throughout he praises the "indescribable innocence and beneficence of Nature" and then in the chapter called "Higher Laws" says that "Nature" (the "animal" part of humanity) is evil and must be suppressed; nature is "hard to be overcome, but she must be overcome."

IS THE LANGUAGE OF THE WORK APPEALING?

The appeal of an author's use of language, especially if it is prose rather than poetry, may be hard to define. The writer may be especially adept at imitating the rhythms of spoken speech, at using internal rhyme, at choosing apt and delightful words, at building suspenseful sentences, at making witty or striking analogies. Emerson and Thoreau are famous, for example, for their pithy, rhetorical phrasing. We expect the language of poetry to be appealing, but one test of the quality of any work is the ability of its language to grip us. The stories and novels of F. Scott Fitzgerald may sometimes seem trivial but they are wonderfully, charmingly written. The attractiveness of a work's language helps make it "good."

DOES THE AUTHOR PRESENT HIS OR HER WORLD VIVIDLY AND INTENSELY?

This quality, like compelling language, is difficult to define, but some authors have the ability to imprint their worlds so vividly on our imaginations that no matter how ridiculous those worlds may be, we delight in the mere rendering of them. Poe and Dickens describe scenes that are utter nonsense (Dickens has one of his villains, whose name is "Krook," die of spontaneous combustion) but are so graphic that we enjoy them nonetheless. The energy and virtuosity of a work may give pleasure no matter what the materials.

HOW WELL DOES THE WORK USE GENERIC ELEMENTS?

Are the characters believable? Is the plot plausible? Are the symbols appropriate? These are but a few questions dealing with specific elements in a work. For more detailed discussions of these questions, see Chapters 3 and 4.

7

How to create good essay content

T HE QUALITY OF AN ESSAY rests largely on its content. Although content includes your introduction and conclusion, it consists primarily of the middle or "proof" part of the essay, the part in which you develop and support your thesis. It is in this part of your essay that you either convince or fail to convince the reader of the validity of your ideas. You can take several steps to make the content of your essays good.

SATISFY YOUR AUDIENCE'S NEED FOR CLARITY

As we noted in Chapter 3, you will write better essays if you think of your audience as being not just your instructor but anyone who enjoys literature and has ideas about it. It may be useful to picture your audience as being physically present when you write. This "listener" will need to know certain things, will have questions that need to be answered, will want complex points clarified. Try to anticipate and supply that person's needs.

It must be emphasized that, above all, your audience needs a full and clear explanation of the points you are making about a work of literature. Student writers often ignore this need, especially when they assume that instructors are their only audience. But, in fact, you need to explain fully, completely, and clearly what you think and why you think it. Your readers—including your instructor—cannot read your mind. Assume that they have already read the work or can read it; this means that you need only summarize and paraphrase those parts of the work that clarify and illustrate your points. But if you do not spell out your ideas, your readers may miss them altogether. In being clear, you may feel that you are being childishly obvious, but it is better to be obvious than obscure.

SATISFY YOUR AUDIENCE'S NEED TO BE CONVINCED

The need to be convinced of the merits of your argument is as great for your instructor as for any other reader. Assume that members of your audience want to learn from you, but do not expect them to surrender their own ideas just because you tell them to. Think of them as constantly asking, Why should we believe what you say? Your job is to show them why.

SUPPORT YOUR IDEAS WITH EVIDENCE

Two kinds of evidence are relevant for essays about literature: evidence from primary sources and evidence from secondary sources. Almost always, evidence from primary sources is more valuable and persuasive than from secondary sources. "Primary sources" are the works of literature themselves. If you are writing about *Catcher in the Rye,* then *Catcher in the Rye* is your primary source. If you are writing about Shakespeare's comedies, then all of these works are your primary source. Anything in your primary source is "evidence." Evidence can be quotations, words, incidents, details of setting, descriptions of characters, conflicts within the plot, word sounds, punctuation—anything in the work. Many students get the idea that evidence consists only of quotations from the works. But evidence need not be quotations; sometimes, in fact, your evidence will be stronger if you summarize the scene or event in your own words, emphasizing what is most salient to your point. For example, you might want to explain what the character Sancho Panza (in Cervantes' *Don Quixote*) is like. You might argue that although the other characters think Sancho foolish, he is actually very shrewd. Once you state this thesis, you need to give evidence to support it. You could bring up Sancho's obsessive use of proverbs, showing their aptness in several situations. You could illustrate his shrewd manipulation of Don Quixote's fantasies, as in the scene where he presents an ugly peasant girl to Don Quixote as the fair Dulcinea. You could summarize the wise judicial decisions he makes when he is governor of his "isle." These are all examples— evidence—and you could present most of them without quoting from the novel at all.

A word about your instructor is appropriate here. It may be that you are getting some of your generalizations from him or her and consequently feel that you don't have to support them with evidence. But put yourself in your instructor's place. A conscientious instructor will want to know one thing about you: how creatively and specifically you can think about the work of literature at hand. Your instructor may be flattered that you agree with his or her ideas, but will still want to see that you have arrived at them in the same way he or she has, by making a careful and creative study of the work. You can show your instructor that you have undergone this process in only one way—by giving evidence.

Evidence from "secondary" sources consists of facts and opinions outside the work itself. Facts about the author's life, about the period in which the author lived, about the author's philosophy, about literary history, about other authors, about the audience, about the work's influence, about similarities to other works—these are secondary sources. Opinions about the work held by the author, by his or her contemporaries, by later critics, by your fellow students, by your instructor—these, also, are secondary sources.

Secondary sources are valuable for what they can teach us about the work. They give us information that helps us to form our own opinions. They give us opinions that spur our critical imagination and that broaden our understanding. When we study Hawthorne's fiction, for example, our perception of his themes sharpens when we learn that he was deeply ashamed of his own Puritan ancestors' dire deeds of intolerance. When we learn that Jane Austen used an actual calendar to plot the events of *Pride and Prejudice,* we come to appreciate the care that she used to construct her work. When we compare Shakespeare's sources with his plays, we see his genius for deepening characterization and creating complex philosophical themes.

Use secondary sources, then, to learn as much as you can about a work. Use good secondary sources—accurate histories and biographies, thoughtful interpretations by respected critics. When you write your paper, if facts that you have discovered are relevant to your argument, cite them and your source for them. If a critic makes an especially good point or gives an especially good analysis, summarize his or her ideas and include particularly apt or telling quotations from his or her essay. Think of secondary sources as witnesses on your behalf. But keep in mind that secondary sources are no substitute for evidence in primary sources. Even when you use secondary sources, you should draw your conclusive evidence from primary sources. Chapter 9 (on documentation) explains how to incorporate secondary sources into your essays.

REASON SOUNDLY

All essays that argue a position must rely on sound logic to make their cases convincing. The following are some do's and don'ts that pertain to essays about literature:

1. Give good evidence. You do this by giving evidence that is important, that is representative of all the evidence that bears on your point, and that is abundant enough to allow your point to rest on more than just one or two isolated examples.

2. Account for all the important evidence, especially evidence that contradicts your thesis. If some facts from or about the works seem to fly in the face of your thesis, explain why they don't nullify it.

3. Represent the work accurately. Make sure that you don't misunderstand, misquote, or oversimplify the text. Read carefully.

4. Avoid *non sequiturs*. *Non sequitur* is Latin for "It does not follow." A *non sequitur* is a generalization or conclusion that is not warranted or supported by the facts or premises you have given.

EXAMPLE: Sinclair Lewis satirized American business practices in *Babbitt*. Therefore, he hated America.

5. When you quote or summarize critics, support their ideas with your own analysis of the primary source. Use critics to support your views, but don't assume that your reader will accept their word as true. Give evidence—your own evidence—to establish the validity of their views. See the sample research paper in Chapter 9 for an example of how to do this.

6. Include all the steps in your reasoning. Arguments proceed to their conclusions by establishing key points ("issues"). The omission or refutation of any one of these points lessens the validity of the argument. Be sure to identify and include all the issues of your argument.

> EXAMPLE: By the end of the novel, Frederic Henry is getting tired of Catherine Barkley for three reasons: (1) He yearns to return to the front; (2) he is uncomfortable with Catherine's obsessive attachment to him; and (3) he finds her views about religion upsetting.

In this example, the writer has given thee reasons for his or her thesis. If the writer neglects one reason or fails to develop it adequately, he or she weakens the validity of the thesis.

7. Avoid meaningless generalizations and words impossible to define.

> EXAMPLES: Macbeth is a magnificent character.
> Romeo and Juliet are truly in love.
> Captain Ahab is hateful.
> Ophelia is a source of wonder.
> *Great Expectations* is the best book I have ever read.

8. Make sure you understand crucial words in the primary source. This point is especially applicable to poetry and earlier authors, like Shakespeare and Chaucer. Be sensitive to word usage, and look up words in a good dictionary when you have any doubts about them. The two most authoritative dictionaries are *The Oxford English Dictionary,* ed. James A. H. Murray et al., 13 vols. (Oxford: Oxford University Press, 1933), and *Webster's Third New International Dictionary of the English Language,* unabridged, ed. Philip Babcock Gove (Springfield, Mass.: Merriam, 1966). *The Oxford English Dictionary (OED)* is based on "historical principles"; that is, it describes and gives examples of a word's use over the years. If you

want to know what a word meant to Shakespeare or Chaucer, look it up in the *OED*. The Merriam *Webster's Third New International* is a "descriptive" dictionary; that is, it describes how the word is used (and spelled) today. The college edition of the Merriam, abridged from the *Third New International,* is adequate for nearly all of your needs, as are most "desk" dictionaries on the market.

9. Don't assume that an author's interpretation of his or her own work is infallible. Sometimes authors discuss their works, but you should question the reliability of such commentary. For example, Mark Twain and William Faulkner talked about their work but were forgetful about what they had actually written and were not above pulling the legs of audiences. Faulkner's comments are fascinating and are in a way extensions of his novels. But to consider them the only correct interpretations of his characters is to limit severely the complexity and meaning of his fiction. Other authors, like Henry James, are more careful when discussing their own work and are thus more reliable. But even here you must beware of making the "intentional fallacy," the assumption that the only valid interpretations of a work are those the author intended. Sometimes an author doesn't entirely know what he intends. Sometimes he or she intends one thing but creates something very different. Sometimes the writer forgets what he or she originally intended and later claims another "intention" for the work. Authors do not have total conscious control of their art, and once they have created a work of literature, they are as much outside it as any sensitive critic, maybe even more so. Although authors' comments on their own work should not be ignored, they should not be taken as the last word.

10. Avoid making biographical information the sole basis for generalizations about an author's work (see point 4, above).

> EXAMPLE: Poe was an alcoholic. Therefore, his nightmarish fiction was a product of alcoholic dreams.

11. Avoid using the words of a character to represent the ideas of the author. Characters are fictional beings. They do not necessarily speak for the author. Thus, David Copperfield does not necessarily speak for Dickens, Nick Adams for Hemingway, Gatsby for Fitzgerald, the "I" of her poems for Emily Dickinson, Nora Helmer for Ibsen.

12. Define key terms. If you want to argue, for example, that Romeo is a "romantic" or that Kathy Ames in John Steinbeck's *East of Eden* is a "psychopath," you need to let your reader know what you mean by those terms. Some terms, like "romantic," don't need a formal definition, but in the course of your essay you need to communicate a specific understanding of how you are using the term. Other terms, like "psychopath," probably do need a formal definition, because they are specialized terms that come from particular disciplines (in this case, psychology).

SAMPLE PARAGRAPHS

Paragraph 1

> Wilfred Owen was a bitter opponent of war. He fought in World War I, and as he fought he became increasingly disillusioned. His poems represent that disillusionment, and one of the most powerful is "Dulce et Decorum Est." In this poem he describes a soldier's death by gas poisoning. In describing this man's death, he shows that war is cruel. So horrible is this death that the speaker has nightmares about it long afterward. Owen concludes his poem by condemning in no uncertain terms those people who have never seen war's tragedy and yet who depict war to their children as glorious. Owen clearly believes that the axiom from Horace, *Dulce et decorum est pro patria mori* ("Sweet and becoming it is to die for one's country"), is a lie. Ironically, only days before the Armistice, Owen was killed in action.

Analysis of paragraph 1

The content of this paragraph is mediocre, even though its general assessment of the poem's viewpoint is correct. The poem does indeed express disillusionment with war. But the paragraph fails to show *how* the poem does so. Even the summary of the events of the poem offers only a vague idea of the details and methods Owen brings to bear on his thesis. The background information (that

Owen fought and died in World War I) is interesting and adds poignancy to the tone and subject matter of the poem, but it is no substitute for evidence from the poem itself. Words and phrases like "war is cruel," "horrible," "nightmares," "no uncertain terms," "war's tragedy" are meaningless unless they are related to the concrete data of Owen's poem. The topic idea of the paragraph is itself vague. The word "disillusionment" could mean a number of things. Compare paragraph 1 with paragraph 2, below.

Paragraph 2

In his poem "Dulce et Decorum Est," Wilfred Owen attacks those people who naïvely glorify war. Such people, he says, have never experienced the horrors of war. If they had, they would not teach their children falsehoods like Horace's *Dulce et decorum est pro patria mori* ("Sweet and decorous it is to die for one's country"). One device Owen uses to develop this point is descriptive imagery. In the first section, he uses visual and aural imagery to describe the physical state of the soldiers. They are "bent double" under heavy packs, "knock-kneed," "coughing," and "drunk with fatigue." Those who have lost their boots walk "bloodshod." They all walk through "sludge." The flares make a "haunting" light in the sky. The men, in other words, have reached their most vulnerable physical and mental state when gas shells drop "softly" behind them. The second section recounts the men's reaction to the gas. In contrast to the first section, in which the physical movements of the men are painfully slow, this section contains frenzied action as the men struggle to get their gas masks on. Owen continues the emphasis on visual and aural imagery. The men yell: "Gas! GAS! Quick, boys!" They undergo an "ecstasy of fumbling" with the masks. But one of the men fails to get his mask on in time, and the speaker sees him through the eerie green fumes of the gas as being "like a man in fire or lime" or like a man drowning "under a green sea." The third section—two lines long—reiterates this visual image, but the words also have an onomatopoetic quality that suggests what the dying man sounds like: "guttering" and "choking." In the last section, the visual and aural images are even harsher. The speaker says that he continues to have nightmares of the soldier's "white eyes writhing in his face" and his blood "gargling from the froth-corrupted lungs." The word "gargling" also imitates the sounds made by the dying man. By this time, Owen can feel sure that the reader sees that dying in war is not "sweet and decorous." Only those who have never been in a war could say that it is.

Analysis of paragraph 2

This paragraph has excellent content. Its topic idea (that Owen attacks false teachings about war) is precise and clear. The writer proceeds to show how Owen achieves this goal. The writer does not discuss every device that Owen uses. These would be for later paragraphs. But he discusses one specific device—descriptive imagery—and does so thoroughly. The writer covers each section of the poem and gives enough examples for the reader to feel that the evidence is typical of the whole work. In general, the writer not only says what the work does but shows how the work does it. The writer allows the reader to experience those concrete parts of the poem that lead to its abstract ideas. This paragraph, furthermore, is twice as long as the first one. The reason is that the writer *needs* this extra length in order to be detailed and thorough. The greater length of paragraph 2, in other words, helps to make its content much better than that of paragraph 1.

8

How to communicate your ideas: Style and organization

A S GOOD AS your essay's content may be, it will be meaningless unless you communicate it well. Effective methods of communication not only get your ideas across to an audience; they also persuade. Perhaps the most effective of these methods are a clear prose style and a coherent plan of organization.

STYLE

Style is the way a writer puts words together in units of thought—sentences—and blends sentences together to make larger units—paragraphs, essays, books. Although your style is a unique expression of your personality, it is more than that. It is also a rhetorical device that helps you to communicate and argue effectively. You should, then, adjust it to serve best the occasion and audience of your essays. Closely related to style is tone. *Tone* is a writer's attitude toward the material and the readers. You convey tone through style.

Sometimes the occasion and audience of an essay might dictate a very informal style and tone—an address to a dinner party or an essay for a satirical magazine, for example, in which you would speak lightheartedly and colloquially. But most of the time, the occasion for essays about literature is comparatively formal. You should thus write for a broad audience—anyone who might be interested in literature—and fit your style to such an audience. Do everything you can to make your style clear, interesting, and readable: vary sentence structure, avoid the passive voice, emphasize active and specific verbs, eliminate wordiness and unnecessary repetition, base syntax on the natural rhythms of spoken English. Your tone should convey a seriousness of purpose, but it need not be stiffly formal. Since essays about literature involve a degree of personal judgment, you may occasionally use "I," especially when distinguishing your ideas from those of others and stressing the individuality of your views. But, generally, you should write in the third person, avoid colloquialisms, and obey standard rules of usage.

Many rhetoric books offer thorough and practical methods for improving style. Three famous and widely used ones are Strunk and White's *The Elements of Style,* Sheridan Baker's *The Practical Stylist,* and Brooks and Warren's *Modern Rhetoric.*

ORGANIZATION

Organization means the creation of a logical, easy-to-follow plan for your essay—one that introduces your topic, leads the reader through your development of the topic, and finally lets the reader know what your essay has accomplished. An essay's organization consists of a beginning (usually one introductory paragraph), a middle (a series of paragraphs that develop the topic), and an end (usually one concluding paragraph). The building blocks of essay organization are paragraphs. Since essays about literature are almost always arguments, they need a *thesis*—one central point that the essay attempts to prove, a point that unifies the whole essay.

The following are some specific pointers about organizing essays about literature.

1. Give your essay a title that states the topic. The title should include the author's full name and the name of the work. For example: "The Influence of the Jungle in Joseph Conrad's *Heart of Darkness.*"

2. Your introduction (the first paragraph or the first few paragraphs) should state your topic and your intentions. This means that you will be repeating the information already given in your title, but in your introduction you should expand on that information as if your reader has not read the title.

3. The thesis of your essay, as in all essays, is the one overall point that you want to make. It will almost always be your answer to the question implicit in your topic. If your question is, "What causes Pip (in Dickens' *Great Expectations*) to change from an immature to a mature person?" your answer to that question is your thesis. (For example, "Pip becomes a mature person when he learns to accept his lowly origins.") You can almost always state your thesis in a sentence or two.

4. The rest of your essay, except the conclusion, will attempt to prove that thesis. Give your essay unity by excluding everything, especially plot summaries, not relevant to your thesis. Devote at least one fully developed paragraph to each of your main points. Provide adequate transitions between paragraphs so that your reader can follow your line of thought.

5. There are many ways to organize the main body of your essay. Rhetoric books describe traditional rhetorical patterns, such as comparison, classification, and definition. Two methods of organization are especially useful in essays about literature. In *spatial organization,* you discuss elements of the work in the order in which they appear. In *chronological organization,* you discuss elements as they occur in chronological order. Often the spatial and chronological order of a work will be the same. For example, the organization of the sample essay on "Young Goodman Brown" in Chapter 12 is both spatial and chronological. Each paragraph follows Brown deeper into the forest according to the chronology of his journey and according to the sequence in which Hawthorne narrates it. But chronological and spatial order are not always the same. Many works employ devices like stream of consciousness and flashbacks that make spatial narration different from the chronological sequence of events. Detective fiction, which depends on a gradual revelation of past events, is a good example. By organizing your essay spatially or chronologically, you give readers a sense of security about your ability to cover *all* the important details. You are in effect taking them on a systematic journey through territory with which they

are familiar, showing them those things that are important to your argument as you go.

6. Finally, provide a conclusion that summarizes briefly what you have tried to accomplish or that at least reminds the reader of your primary purpose in writing the essay.

SAMPLE ESSAYS

Essay 1

A COMPARISON OF MARY AND WARREN IN ROBERT FROST'S "THE DEATH OF THE HIRED MAN"

The purpose and topic of the essay need to be stated more clearly. This paragraph contains statements of fact rather than a statement of purpose.

Robert Frost in "The Death of the Hired Man" presents two different views of how to respond to human need. Into the home of Mary and Warren comes the derelict hired hand, Silas. Mary and Warren disagree over how to treat him.

This paragraph has no topic idea or topic sentence. The writer gives details from the poem, but the reader cannot see why. What point is the writer making?

Mary tells Warren to "be kind" (1. 7) to Silas. Warren, however, is upset with Silas for having run out on him the year before, when he needed him most. "There's no depending on him," Warren says (1. 17). Mary shushes Warren so Silas won't hear him, but Warren doesn't care if Silas hears or not: "I want him to: he'll have to soon or late" (1. 32).

This paragraph, in contrast to the one above, has too many topic sentences. It needs to have just one. The quotations are merely confusing because the reader doesn't know which topic idea this evidence illustrates.

In my opinion, <u>Mary understands Silas much better than Warren. She is also much more sympathetic than Warren.</u> Her sympathy is like that extended to all people by the Virgin Mary. This may be why Frost chose Mary's name, to underscore this quality. She reminds Warren, for example, of Silas' longstanding argument with the college student Harold Wilson. Warren agrees that Silas is proud of his one accomplishment, building a load of hay:

Also, the writer does not explain how these quotations exemplify either sympathy or understanding, but merely reproduces them.

He bundles every forkful in its place,
And tags and numbers it for future
   reference,
So he can find and easily dislodge it
In the unloading. (ll. 89—92)

Mary then tells Warren that Silas has come home to die: "You needn't be afraid he'll leave you this time" (l. 112).

   One of the things that most upsets Warren is that Silas comes to them rather than going to Silas' brother for help:

This paragraph has no topic sentence or topic idea. The writer is summarizing the plot without relating it to any idea being stated.

Why doesn't he go there? His brother's
   rich,
A somebody—director in the bank. (ll.
   127—128)

But Mary explains that probably there is some misunderstanding between Silas and his brother. Also, she says that Silas is "just the kind that kinsfolk can't abide" (l. 141). He may be "worthless," she argues, but "he won't be made ashamed to please his brother" (ll. 145—146).

Same here.

   The climax of the poem comes when Warren seems to agree reluctantly with Mary that Silas should stay. She tells him to go inside and check on him. He quietly returns and catches up her hand. When she asks him what happened, he replies, simply, "Dead."

In this concluding paragraph, the writer lists a number of differences between Warren and Mary but has not explained or illustrated them. Each of these points deserves a paragraph of explanation and illustration. They should be part of the body of the essay.

   In sum, Warren has many qualities that Mary does not have. He is quick to blame, cynical, and even a little stingy. But most of all he lacks the sympathy, the kindness, and the understanding that Mary has. She seems also to be more imaginative than he. Finally, though, her kindness wins him over to her side. Even though Silas dies, Warren seems ready to do what Mary wants.

Analysis of essay 1

This essay has serious problems of organization. It attempts to compare Mary with Warren, but comparisons must be thorough and systematic. This essay is neither. It makes some general statements about how Warren and Mary are different, but beyond that it does little more than summarize the plot of the poem. The essay desperately needs a plan of organization. More specifically, its introductory paragraph needs a narrowly focused statement of the essay's purpose. The middle paragraphs need topic ideas and topic sentences that will unify the material in them. Quotes and references need to be made relevant to the comparison. The differences listed in the final paragraph need explanation and illustration. They should be incorporated into the body of the essay. As the essay now stands, content is weak because the writer fails to state ideas about the work, to develop them convincingly, and to cover the poem thoroughly and concretely. But a good plan of organization would provide the framework for good content. Compare this essay with the reorganized version that follows.

Essay 2

A COMPARISON OF MARY AND WARREN

IN ROBERT FROST'S "THE DEATH OF THE HIRED MAN"

When Silas, the unreliable hired hand, returns to the farm owned by Mary and Warren in Robert Frost's "The Death of the Hired Man," Mary and Warren immediately disagree about what to do with him. Warren wants to send him packing. Mary wants to keep him on and care for him. The poem recounts their disagreement and in so doing reveals some fundamental differences between them.

The most obvious difference is that Mary is compassionate and Warren is not. The poem continually reveals Mary's pity for the sick and troubled Silas. She tells Warren that she discovered him

> Huddled against the barn-door fast asleep,
> A miserable sight, and frightening, too—. (ll.35–36)

His physical weakness

> hurt my heart the way he lay
> And rolled his old head on that sharp-edged chair-back.
> (ll.147—148)

She sums up his future prospects as bleak and hopeless:

> Poor Silas, so concerned for other folk,
> And nothing to look backward to with pride,
> And nothing to look forward to with hope,
> So now and never any different.   (ll. 99—102)

Mary's pity leads her to certain moral conclusions. She feels that they should not just take Silas in, but should try to protect his pride as well. "Be kind," she tells Warren (l. 7). Warren, in contrast, is touchy about any hint that he has not done right by Silas. Mary's gentle request to be kind produces an almost angry response: "When was I ever anything but kind to him?" (l. 11). He is impatient with Silas' shortcomings and unforgivingly moralistic:

> I told him so last haying, didn't I?
> If he left then, I said, that ended it.

He expresses his bitterness loud and clear and doesn't care if Silas hears (l. 32). He dismisses Silas' plans to "ditch the meadow" as the foolish promises of an insincere old man (ll. 43—46).

What is not so obvious is _why_ Mary is compassionate and Warren is not. Frost offers three reasons, each of which reveals more fundamental differences between the two characters. First, they have a different attitude toward people in general. Warren values people for their usefulness and as a result is ready to cast them off when they are no longer useful. He is a farmer, and he measures people in terms of their ability to help him farm. This explains his bitterness about Silas' leaving the year before just when Warren needed him most. Warren's attitude toward people is most apparent now when Silas returns:

> What good is he? Who else will harbor him
> At his age for the little he can do?
> What help he is there's no depending on.   (ll. 15–17)

Even one of the few positive things Warren can say about Silas
concerns a useful skill, Silas' ability to load hay: "Silas does that
well" (l. 92). Warren believes, then, that the only reason to be
kind to people is that they may be useful to him. Mary's
compassionate reaction to Silas' plight reveals an entirely
different view of people. She sees them as good in themselves.
She admits that Silas may be "worthless" (l. 144) as a hired
hand—

> You'll be surprised at him—how much he's broken.
> His working days are done; I'm sure of it.
>
>   (ll. 152–153)

—but she insists that their farm is his "home," and it is their
responsibility to receive him. Warren's definition of home is in
keeping with his measurement of people in terms of their
usefulness:

> Home is the place where, when you have to go there,
> They have to take you in.   (ll. 118–119)

In other words, home is the place where, when you have become
useless and an imposition, people have to take care of you, not
out of love but out of reluctant and bitter duty. Mary's counter-
definition is in keeping with her assessment of people as
valuable in themselves:

> I should have called it
> Something you somehow haven't to deserve.
>   (ll. 119–120)

In other words, people should not have to earn tenderness by
being useful. They should receive tenderness just because they
are people. And "home" should provide that tenderness lovingly
and selflessly. Mary sees their farm as Silas' home.

A second reason for the difference in their attitudes toward Silas is that Mary is imaginative and Warren is not. Frost suggests this quality in the opening line of the poem: "Mary sat musing on the lamp-flame at the table." The word "muse" means "to ponder or meditate," "to consider reflectively." The word is associated with the Muses of Greek mythology, "each of whom presided over a different art or science." Because of this association, the noun "muse" means "the spirit or power regarded as inspiring and watching over poets, musicians, and artists; a source of inspiration" (The American Heritage Dictionary of the English Language [New York: American Heritage Publishing Co., 1969]). Frost's use of the term introduces Mary as something of a poet. She at least has the reflective and imaginative capacity of a poet. By using her imagination, she can put herself in the place of others and experience what they feel. Her imagination allows her to "understand" Silas. She guesses why he says he wants to ditch the meadow, even though he probably knows he cannot:

> Surely you wouldn't grudge the poor old man
> Some humble way to save his self-respect.   (ll. 49–50)

She understands why Silas remains troubled by his arguments with the college boy Harold Wilson:

> I sympathize. I know just how it feels
> To think of the right thing to say too late.   (ll. 76–77)

She realizes that "he has come home to die" (l. 111). Warren, in contrast, lacks the imagination to see past his own practical and rather selfish needs. Frost doesn't suggest that Warren's needs are invalid or unimportant; he shows, rather, that Warren cannot see beyond them. And this limited vision causes him to be unsympathetic to people who hinder them. When Warren asks somewhat stingily why Silas' brother ("a somebody—director in the bank," l. 129) can't take care of Silas, Mary has to tell him that the banker-brother may not want to take Silas in. When Warren wonders why, Mary has to tell him why. She uses her imagination to guess what the trouble may be:

> He don't know why he isn't quite as good
> As anybody. Worthless though he is,
> He won't be made ashamed to please his brother.   (ll.
> 143–145)

Their different imaginative capacities lead them to different ethical conclusions. Warren wants to do unto others according to their effect on his self-centered needs. Mary wants to do unto others as she would be done by were she in their place. Through her imagination she can feel what "their place" is like.

A third cause of their different attitudes toward Silas is that Mary is allied to nature and Warren is not. Frost directly connects Mary to nature twice. Just before Mary and Warren exchange definitions of "home," Frost describes nature in highly metaphoric terms:

> Part of a moon was falling down the west,
> Dragging the whole sky with it to the hills.
> Its light poured softly in her lap.   (ll. 103–105)

It is indicative of the kind of person Mary is that she responds to this fanciful and beautiful quality in nature. And her response seems to cause or at least to fortify her compassionate impulses:

> She saw it
> And spread her apron to it. She put out her hand
> Among the harp-like morning-glory strings,
> Taut with the dew from the garden bed to eaves,
> As if she played unheard some tenderness
> That wrought on him beside her in the night.   (ll.
> 105–110)

Frost's second connection of Mary with nature occurs at the end, when Mary sends Warren to "see for yourself" how Silas is. She urges him once again to be kind and then says that as she waits for his return she will

> see if that small sailing cloud
> Will hit or miss the moon.   (ll.160–161)

Frost actually blends her in with nature: the cloud

>   hit the moon.
> Then there were three there, making a dim row,
> The moon, the little silver cloud, and she.   (ll. 161–163)

Mary's sympathy with nature, like her view of humankind and her active imagination, also leads to ethical conclusions. They should be merciful to Silas just as they would be to any other living creature:

> Of course he's nothing to us, any more
> Than was the hound that came a stranger to us
> Out of the woods, worn out upon the trail.   (ll. 115–117)

Her point is that they should care for Silas for the same reason they cared for the stray dog: both are living creatures. Frost does not say anything about Warren's attitude toward nature, but Warren's not saying anything is in itself suggestive that he lacks Mary's poetic love for nature. We can infer that to Warren, nature is meant to be used. He is a farmer, and as such he seems to have reduced nature to its economic value, just as he has done with people.

We might wonder why, if Warren and Mary are so different, they ever got married. But as it turns out, Warren is not quite so different from Mary as he at first seems. It is true that he lacks her positive view of people, her imagination, her sympathy for nature, and thus her compassion. But he is not confined irretrievably in a hard shell of selfish indifference. He is persuadable. Who knows, he may have married Mary just for her imaginative and compassionate qualities. By the end of their conversation (and the poem), at least, he has come around to her view. He is now sympathetic to Silas and takes his side against the status-minded brother: "I can't think Si ever hurt anyone" (l. 146). He even argues that maybe Silas' working days aren't over after all (l. 154). And when he brings news of Silas' death, he does so as Mary would have, with solemnity and tenderness.

Analysis of essay 2

This is an excellent essay. It has a logical and easy-to-follow plan of organization, which in turn leads to concrete, thorough and convincing content. The first paragraph clearly introduces the topic of the essay: Mary and Warren's different attitudes toward Silas. The second paragraph explains the general way in which they are different. The ensuing paragraphs explain three specific points of difference. The plan of organization is simple: to take one point of difference at a time and explain and illustrate it thoroughly. Note that each of the paragraphs in the body of the essay deals with one of these points of difference and announces its point with an unmissable topic sentence (these are underlined in the essay). The final paragraph brings the essay to a close by summarizing the differences between Mary and Warren and by introducing the similarity between them that brings their relationship to a point of harmony at the end of the poem.

9

How to document sources

DOCUMENTATION, OR "GIVING CREDIT," means identifying the sources you consult when you prepare your essays. When you write essays about literature, you must use at least one source—the primary source, the work of literature itself. You may also want to use secondary sources. (For a full discussion of primary and secondary sources, see the section on "Evidence," beginning on page 90.)

RESEARCH PAPERS AND THE USE OF SECONDARY SOURCES

Most people associate the use of secondary sources with "research" and "research papers," so a word is appropriate here about what research papers are. In literary studies, there are essentially two kinds of research papers. The first kind reports on background or biographical information that illuminates works of literature. The job of the researcher here is to gather the facts, give order to them, and report them accurately. An example might be a paper on a work's critical reception or on an event in an author's life, such as the financial crisis that struck Mark Twain late in his career and increased the bitterness of his writings.

The second kind of research paper offers an interpretation of a literary work or works. The writer searches through secondary sources in order to find facts and opinions that will help to establish a reasonable interpretation, or perhaps even a new one. Some research papers try to represent as many different views on a work as possible. Others use only a few secondary sources, either to support and illuminate their own ideas or as springboards for alternative interpretations. The sample essay on E. A. Robinson's "Richard Cory" in Chapter 12, for example, takes issue with one critic's opinion in order to present another view.

The most important point to remember about research papers is that, for all their use of sources, they are still *essays*. Like all essays, a research paper should represent the writer's opinions about his or her subject. A research paper, then, should be a synthesis of *your* discoveries about a topic and *your* evaluation of those discoveries. It should not be a mere anthology of other people's ideas or of facts. It should have what all good essays have: a unifying idea expressed directly and emphatically in a thesis; an introduction and a conclusion; and paragraphs that relate to the essay's thesis and that follow logically from one another. The sample essay at the end of this chapter exemplifies these traits.

GUIDELINES FOR FINDING INFORMATION AND OPINION ABOUT LITERATURE

Your research needs will vary from writing project to writing project. Some projects will require minimal research, others more elaborate research. Let's say, however, that you have to write an essay about a particular work. Your instructor requires only that you use the primary source, but you want to do some outside reading to get yourself thinking about the work. Go, then, to the card catalog of your college library, find where the author's works are in the stacks, and browse among the books in that section. In a good library, there will be many books about well-known authors. So choose a few of the books that look promising for your needs, look up the work you will be writing about in the indexes, and read what each book has to say about the work. If, for example, you are interested in an important poem by Browning, a book that surveys all of Browning's works will have several pages on your poem. It should take you only a few minutes to read through what you find.

Your purpose in doing this kind of exploratory and casual reading is to familiarize yourself with critics' assessment of the characteristics and themes of the work. This knowledge should stimulate your thoughts and get you started on your essay. If it turns out that you want to incorporate some of this material in your essay or that your teacher does in fact require you to use a few secondary sources, then you should read carefully in these books, take notes, and, in your essay, give credit for your sources.

However, what if there is very little in the stacks on your author, or what if your teacher asks you to do a full-fledged research paper? It may be that you will be lucky enough to find plenty of material in the stacks—biography, background information, criticism—but you will probably need to supplement that material with what you turn up in a second place in the library, the reference room. The reference room is especially helpful when books are missing from the stacks (lost or checked out) or your library's collection on a particular author is small.

The reference room of a college library typically provides several kinds of materials. First, it contains books with background information. These include encyclopedias, literary histories, books containing brief biographies, books that describe and illustrate critical reactions to authors, handbooks to literary terms, surveys of contemporary authors and their works, guides to works by ethnic minorities. The "Oxford Companion" series published by the Oxford University Press (the *Oxford Companion to American Literature,* the *Oxford Companion to English Literature,* the *Oxford Companion to the Theatre,* and so forth) is an example of this kind of book. So, too, is the *Encyclopaedia Britannica,* which has, among other things, fine essays on authors and literary movements. Second, the reference room contains books that give specific and specialized information about primary sources. These include concordances and indexes to standard authors like Tennyson, Milton, and Shakespeare as well as books dealing with specialized qualities of works, like their use of allusions, Greek mythology, or the Bible.

A third kind of material typical of reference rooms is bibliographies. With these, you can make your research systematic and thorough. Three bibliographies should be very useful to you and should probably be the first you consult:

> *Literary History of the United States.* Ed. Robert E. Spiller et
> al. 4th ed. rev. New York: Macmillan, 1974. Vol. II. (Vol.
> I is the literary history; Vol. II is the bibliography.)
> *MLA International Bibliography of Books and Articles on the Mod-*
> *ern Languages and Literatures.* New York: Modern Lan-
> guage Association, 1922—.
> *The New Cambridge Bibliography of English Literature.* Ed.
> George Watson. 5 vols. Cambridge: Cambridge Univ.
> Press, 1969–1977.

Between them, the *LHUS* and the *New CBEL* bibliographies
cover all of English and American literature up through the modern
period. They cover movements, historical periods, and authors.
They are "selective" bibliographies in that they list the most important writings by and about authors. In other words, they save you
time by weeding out unimportant and repetitive books and essays.
The *MLA International Bibliography* is published annually and covers
everything published each year on "modern languages, literature,
folklore, and linguistics." To find what you need in the *MLA International Bibliography,* look up your author's country and the period
in which he or she has written. Authors are listed alphabetically
within periods; works are listed alphabetically under authors.

Probably you will find all you need in the *New CBEL* and the
LHUS bibliographies, but like all bibliographies, these are dated.
That is, they cover what has been written up to their dates of pub-
lication. To cover work done after these dates, consult the *MLA
International Bibliography.*

In addition to these three bibliographies, you might find
some others helpful. There are individual bibliographies for almost
every major author, and in contrast to the *New CBEL* and the
LHUS bibliographies, these usually list everything written by and
about an author. Also, the *Readers' Guide to Periodical Literature* and
the *Book Review Digest* list articles and reviews in newspapers and
popular journals. Finally, there are the bibliographies of broad categories of literature, such as the novel, the short story, and drama.
These bibliographies point you to the major criticism on specific
works. To use these bibliographies, look up the work in the appropriate bibliography; there you will find a list of critical essays on
the work you are studying. These bibliographies undergo constant

revision, so check for supplements that bring them up to date. You can bring them up to date yourself with the *MLA International Bibliography*. A few examples are as follows:

> *The Contemporary Novel: A Checklist of Critical Literature on the British and American Novel since 1945*. Comp. Irving Adelman and Rita Dworkin. Metuchen, N.J.: Scarecrow Press, 1972.
>
> *The Continental Novel: A Checklist of Criticism in English 1900–1966*. Comp. E. I. Kearney and L. S. Fitzgerald. Metuchen, N.J.: Scarecrow Press, 1968.
>
> *Dramatic Criticism Index: A Bibliography of Commentaries on Playwrights from Ibsen to the Avant-Garde*. Comp. Paul F. Breed and Florence M. Sniderman. Detroit: Gale Research, 1972.
>
> *English Novel Explication: Criticism to 1972*. Comp. Helen H. Palmer and Anne Jane Dyson. Hamden, Conn.: Shoe String Press, 1973. *Supplement I* (1976).
>
> *European Drama Criticism: 1900 to 1975*. Comp. Helen H. Palmer. 2nd ed. Hamden, Conn.: Shoe String Press, 1977.
>
> *Greek and Roman Authors: A Checklist of Criticism*. Comp. Thomas Gwinup and Fidelia Dickinson. Metuchen, N.J.: Scarecrow Press, 1973.
>
> *A Guide to Critical Reviews: Part I: American Drama, 1909–69*. Comp. James Salem. 2nd ed. Metuchen, N.J.: Scarecrow Press, 1972.
>
> *Poetry Explication: A Checklist of Interpretation since 1925 of British and American Poems Past and Present*. Comp. Joseph Kuntz and Nancy Martinez. 3rd ed. Boston: G. K. Hall, 1980.
>
> *Twentieth-Century Short Story Explication: Interpretations 1900–1975, of Short Fiction since 1800*. Comp. Warren S. Walker. 3rd ed. Hamden, Conn.: Shoe String Press, 1977. *Supplement I* (1980).

By consulting these bibliographies, you can draw up a thorough list of books and journal articles about an author. But you probably won't have time to read all of these books and articles, so unless your instructor wants a comprehensive list, list only those items that seem most interesting and most relevant to your topic.

Then check to see if your library has the books on your list. If not or if the books are checked out, move on to the journal articles. One advantage of journal articles is that, if your library subscribes to the journals, almost certainly they cannot be checked out. They should, in other words, be available for your use. To find the article, you need to go to a third place in the library, the periodicals room. Ask the periodicals librarian to help you find the journal you need. These will usually be bound and located in the stacks or will be on microfilm. You can also check the "Serials Holding Catalog" to see whether your library subscribes to the journal and to discover its call number and thus its location.

The information provided here about finding information and opinion about works of literature is basic and should serve almost all of your research needs while you are in college. If you want more thorough guidance on a particular project, or if you are interested in learning more about the methods of literary research, you might consult the following excellent book:

> Richard Altick and Andrew H. Wright, eds. *Selective Bibliography for the Study of English and American Literature*. 5th ed. New York: Macmillan, 1974.

But perhaps the most valuable resource for doing research is the reference librarian. Reference librarians are experts on locating sources of information and opinion. They are usually eager to help. And they can save you time.

GIVING CREDIT: WHY, WHEN, AND WHERE

Why should you give credit?

There are several reasons for giving credit to your sources. One is to give readers information that allows them to find and read the same material you read. They may also want to check the reliability of your sources or your ability to use them fairly and accurately. Giving credit, to put it positively, is one more means of arguing. The more careful and honest you are in giving credit, the stronger your argument will be. Another reason for giving credit is to distinguish your ideas from those of others. The purpose of the essay, after all, is to express your ideas, to argue your position. You may use facts, ideas, and words from other sources to clarify and support your ideas, but readers are interested, finally, in knowing what you think. That is why they are reading your paper. By giving credit, both in your text and in footnotes, you show them exactly where your ideas begin and where other writers' ideas leave off.

The most obvious reason for giving credit is to adhere to an ethical standard. Student honor policies stress this reason heavily. But although the ethical principle is obvious, it is not always simple. The usual definition of *plagiarism* is "the presentation of someone else's ideas, work, or facts as your own." The moral judgment that follows is, "Plagiarism is stealing and therefore wrong." These judgments are adequate when applied to blatant plagiarism, cases in which someone copies, verbatim or almost verbatim, the work of someone else and claims it as his or her own. Most cases of student plagiarism, however, are not so obvious or so consciously criminal. The issue of plagiarism is clouded with some uncertainties. Everything you know, for example, comes from a "source." When is what you know "yours" and not someone else's? Another uncertainty is that when you summarize someone else's ideas, you will probably use some of that writer's words. How many and what kind of words can you use without plagiarizing? A third uncertainty is the nature of facts. Some facts, even when they appear in a source, do not need documentation. But which ones? Because of uncertainties like these, most students who "plagiarize" do so unconsciously. The following are principles and guidelines that anyone using sources in essays about literature should obey. They should help you to use sources usefully, clearly, and ethically.

When should you give credit?

1. <u>Give credit for primary sources.</u> Whenever you make a specific reference to an incident or words in a work and whenever you quote from a work, you need to give credit to the source from which you obtained the information. This is as true for primary as for secondary sources. You must do this for several reasons. Works of literature, especially famous ones, often go through

many editions and even different publishing houses. Readers need to know which edition you are using so that they can refer to the parts of the work you discuss. You document your primary source, then, for their convenience. But another reason is that the edition you use may affect the validity of your argument. If the edition is unscholarly and contains misprints or omissions, then your interpretations will be suspect. A famous example is Emily Dickinson's poetry. After the poet's death, Thomas Wentworth Higgenson and Mabel Loomis Todd edited her poetry for publication. Instead of publishing it as it had been written, however, they "regularized" it for the tastes of nineteenth-century readers. They changed the meter to make it more conventional, they changed words to make them rhyme, they normalized punctuation. Not until Thomas H. Johnson published his edition of her poems in 1955 did we have Emily Dickinson's poetry as she wrote it. If you write an essay about Emily Dickinson's poetry, your readers will want to know that you used Johnson's edition (or reprints from Johnson's edition). By giving full information about the edition you use, you enhance the reliability of your essay.

Often the nature of a college course allows you to omit complete citations for primary sources. You may be writing about a work that appears in one of your course textbooks. If so, the number of the page on which each quotation or specific reference occurs is usually all the documentation you need. Give the quotation or reference and then follow it with the page number or numbers in parentheses, placing your final mark of punctuation after the closing parenthesis.

EXAMPLE (a quote): Lawrence says that when she is with her children she feels "the center of her heart go hard" (p. 125).

EXAMPLE (a specific reference but not a quote): When she returns home from the party, she finds Paul riding the rocking horse. Lawrence contrasts her elegant, even icy dress with Paul's frenzied and exhausted state (pp. 134–135).

More formal usage, however, requires that you give a complete citation for the edition you are using as soon as you make a reference to it (see the section in this chapter on footnotes).

This practice is always necessary when you use a book that is not a basic text in your course.

2. <u>Give credit for facts that are not common knowledge.</u> "Common knowledge" facts are those that the average well-read person would be likely to know. They include very basic facts about history (say, that Lincoln was President of the United States during the American Civil War), birth and death dates, occupations, publication dates, basic biographical facts about famous people (that Lincoln was a rail splitter, that he married Mary Todd, that he debated Stephen A. Douglas, that he ran for the Senate against Douglas and lost, that he chose U. S. Grant to direct the Union Army). Facts that aren't common knowledge have to come from sources (what Lincoln actually said in his debates with Douglas, what conditions led to his defeat, what his personal opinions about Grant were), and those sources must be cited. Also, facts that are in any way controversial need to be documented. If you state that Theodore Roosevelt was a secret Marxist, or had an affair with Emma Goldman, or conspired to assassinate President McKinley, you must give sources (assuming that any exist!) for these assertions; otherwise your reader will write you off as a crank.

3. <u>Give credit for all direct quotes.</u> This kind of documentation is crucial, whether you quote from primary or secondary sources.

4. <u>Give credit for summaries or paraphrases</u> of someone else's ideas. Even when you don't quote directly from the work, you must provide documentation for the sources of your summaries or paraphrases of someone else's ideas. This includes ideas held by other writers, by your instructor, or even by other students. It also includes ideas that you arrive at on your own and then find expressed in print.

5. <u>Give credit for ideas not "assimilated"</u> by you. Once you have absorbed someone's ideas, thought about them over a period of time, added thoughts of your own or of others, you can assume that these ideas are now "yours." If, however, your memory is so good that these ideas remain in your mind exactly as they were when you read and heard them, then you must give credit to the original author.

Where should you give credit?

1. <u>Give credit in the text of your essay.</u> When you use the ideas and facts of another person, acknowledge them *in your own text,* not just in a footnote. To do this, use introductory phrases like the following:

> As Lionel Trilling says, "the ground for complaint . . ."
> One critic has noted "the absurdity of Huck's shore experience."
> Robert E. Spiller suggests . . .
> Tuchman's second point is . . .
> Leo Marx's theory about technology in America is . . .

All of these introduce paraphrases, summaries, and short quotes. The following example introduces an indented (that is, a long) quote. (For a complete explanation of handling quotations, see Chapter 10.)

> In defending his novel, Wright made the following observation: . . .

Acknowledgments for facts are necessary, too, when the facts are very specialized or controversial. For example, details about F. Scott Fitzgerald's love life in Hollywood during his last years can come from only a few people. You must mention such people *in your text* when you use them:

> Sheilah Graham claims that . . .
> Budd Schulberg saw that Fitzgerald was . . .
> Nathanael West said that at the party Fitzgerald concentrated his attention on . . .

Note, however, that facts available from many sources do not need textual acknowledgment. Details about English history, for example, are available in many textbooks and are not associated with any one person or group. They would need only a footnote.

Technically, the failure to acknowledge sources *in your text* is plagiarism. This is true even when you footnote adequately.

2. <u>Give credit in footnotes.</u> The word "footnote" is misleading. "Citation" is more accurate because footnotes no longer usually appear at the foot of the page. In fact, in informal usage a footnote (in the form of a full citation) can appear in the text itself, a practice that eliminates the need for numbers and that makes the citation immediately available to the reader.

> EXAMPLE: As Jay Martin says in *Harvests of Change: American Literature 1865–1914* (Englewood Cliffs, N.J.: Prentice-Hall, 1967), Robinson, "fearful of the responsibilities that were pressing upon him, believed he could not live beyond thirty-five" (p. 154).

Subsequent references to Martin's book would follow standard footnote form except that you would put them in the text and not use footnote numbers.

> EXAMPLE: Martin further points out that Robinson suffered near deafness from a mastoid infection and almost lost his sight in 1893 (Martin, p. 143).

In more formal usage, footnotes should be numbered and placed at the end of the essay. Only essays that will be photocopied (microfilmed) really need footnotes at the bottom of each page. Such practice is common for Master's theses and Ph.D. dissertations. But your instructor may prefer that you do yours this way, so check with him or her.

What information should be in a footnote? The answer is, everything your reader needs to know in order to find the work and the exact location of your reference or quotation. A footnote should include at least the author's name (if you haven't already mentioned it in the text), the name of his or her work, where the work was published, who published it, when it was published, and the page (or pages) on which your reference occurs. Other information is sometimes necessary, but these items are basic. They answer the obvious questions: Who? What? When? Where?

3. <u>Give credit in a bibliography.</u> Most college essays about literature do not need bibliographies. Even scholarly articles rarely use bibliographies. The reason is that footnotes usually provide

an easily read list of sources; a bibliography would be superfluous. Sometimes, however, you need a bibliography. See, for example, the useful bibliography in the sample essay at the end of this chapter.

Include a bibliography when

a. Your instructor asks you to.

b. You have many sources and an alphabetical listing of them would be convenient for your readers.

c. You want to cite works that you have consulted but that do not appear in your footnotes. Include these items in your bibliography as well as the works you *have* cited in your footnotes.

CORRECT FOOTNOTE FORM

Footnote form varies from discipline to discipline. For people writing about literature, the authoritative guide to footnote and bibliographical form is the *MLA Handbook For Writers of Research Papers, Theses, and Dissertations.*

The following are basic footnote patterns as established in the *MLA Handbook.* Most likely, the forms given here are all you will need for college essays. But when in doubt about a particular entry, check with your instructor or consult the *Handbook,* which covers every possible nuance and variation of footnote form. Your library or your instructor will have a copy of the *Handbook.* You may even want one for yourself; buy or order one from your college bookstore.

Footnote appearance

1. <u>Numbers.</u> Footnote numbers are Arabic. A number immediately follows the reference and is raised slightly above the line.

> EXAMPLE: J. H. Plumb claims that the American Revolution had been prophesied long before it occurred.[1]

A corresponding number appears immediately before the footnote and is also raised slightly above the line. (The *MLA Handbook* calls for a space between footnote number and first word, but either way—space or no space—is correct.)

> [1]*England in the Eighteenth Century* (Baltimore, Md.: Penguin, 1950), p. 130.

Number your footnotes consecutively, no matter how many you have. Note that when you mention the author's name in your text, you need not repeat it in the footnote. You should, however, repeat the title of the work even if you mention it in the text.

2. <u>Indentation.</u> Indent the first line of each footnote five spaces, just as you would a paragraph. The rest of the footnote goes all the way to the margins, just as in a paragraph.

3. <u>Spacing.</u> Single-space footnotes. Double-space between them. (This is the usual style for college essays. The *MLA Handbook* specifies that endnotes—notes placed at the back of the essay—should be double-spaced and that footnotes—notes placed at the bottom of the page—be single-spaced. If your teacher prefers that you double-space endnotes, do so. But single-spacing is more usual and is equally correct.)

Footnoting books

1. <u>Book with one author.</u>

> [2]Daniel Hoffman, *Poe Poe Poe Poe Poe Poe* (Garden City, N.Y.: Doubleday, 1972), p. 47.

This is the basic footnote form for books. Note the punctuation. Note that the author's name is in normal order—last name last, first name first. (You put last names first only in alphabetical lists.)

2. <u>First reference to a primary source.</u>

³Maria Edgeworth, *Castle Rackrent* (New York: Norton, 1965), p. 5. Further references to this work will appear in parentheses in the text.

The second sentence of this footnote saves you from having to footnote the work every time you refer to it. This is standard procedure for citing primary sources. Note that the date of publication refers to the year when the current publisher, Norton, published the book, not when Maria Edgeworth first published it.

3. A book with two authors.

⁴Lester V. Berry and Melvin Van den Bark, *The American Thesaurus of Slang: With Supplement* (New York: Crowell, 1947), pp. 50–55.

4. A translation.

⁵Miguel de Cervantes Saavedra, *The Adventures of Don Quixote,* trans. J. M. Cohen (Baltimore, Md.: Penguin, 1950), p. 932.

5. A book that has three authors or more, has gone through several editions, and is one of several volumes in a set.

⁶Robert E. Spiller et al., *Literary History of the United States,* 4th ed. rev. (New York: Macmillan, 1974), I, 143.

Note that the abbreviation for "page" or "pages" ("p." or "pp.") is omitted when preceded by a volume number. As for the abbreviation "et al." (*et alii,* Latin for "and others"), you may use it after the first author's name if there are more than three authors. The alternative is to give all the authors' names.

6. An introduction to a primary source.

⁷William Charvat, Introd., *The Last of the Mohicans,* by James Fenimore Cooper (Boston: Riverside Press, 1958), p. xvii.

7. <u>An edition of an author's work.</u>

> [8]John Dryden, *The Best of Dryden,* ed. Louis I. Bredvold (New York: Ronald Press, 1933), p. 243.

8. <u>An anonymous introduction in an anthology of literature.</u>

> [9]"The Middle Ages (to 1485)," in *The Norton Anthology of English Literature,* ed. M. H. Abrams et al., rev. (New York: Norton, 1968), I, 23.

Footnoting articles in scholarly journals

> [10]Daniel G. Hoffman, "Irving's Use of American Folklore in 'The Legend of Sleepy Hollow,'" *PMLA,* 68 (June 1953), 425.

This is the basic form for footnoting articles in scholarly journals. The information supplied is the author's name, the title of the article, the name of the journal, the volume number, the month and year of publication, and the page number. Note that the abbreviation for "page" or "pages" ("p." or "pp.") is omitted when the page number follows a volume number. Sometimes volume numbers are put in Roman numerals; here, then, the volume could be "LXVIII." But many writers prefer Arabic numerals because they are easier to read.

Footnoting articles in popular publications

1. <u>A weekly magazine.</u>

> [11]Gordon Rogoff, "The Mere Human Props of Eugene O'Neill," *Saturday Review,* 28 May 1977, p. 38.

2. <u>A monthly magazine.</u>

> [12]Michael Malone, "Books in Brief," *Harper's,* June 1977, pp. 83–84.

3. A book review in a weekly magazine.

[13]Ormond Seavey, "Adventures and True Believers,"
rev. of *Prophetic Waters: The River in Early American Life
and Literature*, by John Seelye, *The Nation*, 11 June 1977,
p. 728.

4. An article in a newspaper. The page reference includes the section of the newspaper as well as the page and column numbers.

[14]Joseph McLellan, "'Il Trovatore' at Wolf Trap: Warming the Wind," *The Washington Post*, 8 June 1977, Sec. B,
p. 7, col. 3.

Content footnotes

[15]You can use footnotes to give additional information
or opinion. This footnote looks like any other footnote except
that it contains your words rather than details about sources.
You can also use content footnotes to give further quotations.

Making subsequent references to secondary sources

When making references to a work after you have given a complete
citation for it, give enough information to identify it clearly and
exactly. Usually the author's last name and the page number(s) are
adequate.

[16]Charvat, p. xviii.
[17]Plumb, pp. 41−42.

If you use more than one work by an author, give his or her
last name, enough of the title to identify it, and the page reference.
Avoid such abbreviations as *ibid.* and *op. cit.*; they often create ambiguity.

[18]Hoffman, "Irving's Use of American Folklore," p. 426.
[19]Hoffman, *Poe*, p. 48.

Making subsequent references to primary sources

1. <u>Fiction and nonfiction.</u> Do not use footnotes after your first footnote reference to a primary source. Instead, give page numbers in parentheses in your text. The following is an example of a first reference to a primary source:

> [20]Thomas Mann, "Disorder and Early Sorrow," *Stories of Three Decades,* trans. H. T. Lowe-Porter (New York: Knopf, 1936), p. 501. Further page references to this story will appear in parentheses in the text.

A subsequent reference would be as follows:

> Mann says that Prof. Cornelius sees the past as "dead" and thus "immortalized" (p. 506).

Note that the parentheses come immediately after the quote and the quotation mark. Any mark of punctuation that belongs to the quote, like a question mark or exclamation point, would be included within the quotation marks. But marks of punctuation that belong to *your* sentence—a period, semicolon, comma—come after the parentheses.

> EXAMPLE: Hawkeye exclaims, "Rivenoak came on board yesterday?" (p. 101).
> EXAMPLE: Why does Hawkeye think that Judith is "morally deficient" (p. 76)?

When the quotation is indented, however, put the parenthetical page reference after *all* marks of punctuation.

> EXAMPLE: Hawthorne suggests the symbolic value of the House of Seven Gables in these words:
>
> > But as for the old structure of our story, its white-oak frame, and its boards, shingles, and crumbling plaster, and even the huge, clustered chimney in the midst, seemed to constitute only the least and meanest part of its reality. So much of mankind's varied experi-

> ence had passed there—so much had been suffered,
> and something, too, enjoyed—that the very timbers
> were oozy, as with the moisture of the heart. It was
> itself like a great human heart, with a life of its own,
> and full of rich and sombre reminiscences. (p. 27)

This rule applies to parenthetical references for poetry and plays as well as for fiction and nonfiction. For extensive examples of how parenthetical references are handled, see the sample essays in Chapter 12.

2. Poetry. After your first footnote, give line numbers in parentheses in your text if the poem is long (over about twenty lines).

> EXAMPLE—one line: (1. 75).
> EXAMPLE—two or more lines: (11. 86—90).

If the poem is short, the reader should have no trouble finding the reference. Thus you need not indicate line or page numbers.

3. Plays. If the play is in poetry, give act, scene, and line numbers in parentheses in your text.

> EXAMPLE: (IV, iii, 24—28)

If you are discussing more than one play, give the name of the play as well.

> EXAMPLE: (*Othello* III, ii, 49)

If the play is in prose, give the page number in parentheses in your text, as you would for fiction.

CORRECT BIBLIOGRAPHY FORM

Entries in bibliographies contain nearly the same information as footnotes but follow a different form and method of arrangement. As with footnote form, the source of the following rules is the *MLA Handbook.*

General rules

1. Arrange entries alphabetically by author. If the author is anonymous, list the entry by its title.
2. Do not number entries.
3. Put the author's last name first.
4. Put the first line flush with the left margin. Indent the rest of the entry five spaces.
5. Include without exception every source cited in your essay.
6. When you include more than one work by one author, substitute ten hyphens for the author's name after the first citation.

> EXAMPLE:
> Jewett, Sarah Orne. *A Country Doctor.* New York: Garrett
>   Press, 1970.
> ----------. *A White Heron and Other Stories.* Boston: Houghton
>   Mifflin, 1886.

7. Mentally divide your entries into three main sections: author's name (with the last name first), the name of the article or book, and information about publication. End each of these sections with a period. Note the punctuation and arrangement of the following entries: compare them with the footnote forms for these same sources in the preceding section. See also the bibliography that follows the sample research paper (p. 137).

Sample bibliographic entries for books

1. <u>Book with one author</u>.

> Hoffman, Daniel. *Poe Poe Poe Poe Poe Poe.* Garden City,
>   N.Y.: Doubleday, 1972.

2. <u>A book with two authors</u>.

> Berry, Lester V., and Melvin Van den Bark. *The American
>   Thesaurus of Slang: With Supplement.* New York:
>   Crowell, 1947.

3. A translation.

> Cervantes Saavedra, Miguel de. *The Adventures of Don Quixote.* Trans. J. M. Cohen. Baltimore, Md.: Penguin, 1950.

4. A book that has three authors or more, has gone through several editions, and is one of several volumes in a set.

> Spiller, Robert E., et al. *Literary History of the United States.* 4th ed. rev. New York: Macmillan, 1974. Vol. I.

5. An introduction to a primary source.

> Charvat, William, introd. *The Last of the Mohicans.* By James Fenimore Cooper. Boston: Riverside Press, 1958.

6. An edition of an author's work.

> Dryden, John. *The Best of Dryden.* Ed. Louis I. Bredvold. New York: Ronald Press, 1933.

7. An anonymous introduction in an anthology of literature.

> "The Middle Ages (to 1485)." In *The Norton Anthology of English Literature.* Ed. M. H. Abrams et al. Rev. New York: Norton, 1968, I, 1–25.

Note that when you cite sections of books, you usually give numbers for the whole section. An exception is the introduction to an entire book, as in the example above.

Sample bibliographic entry for articles in scholarly journals

> Hoffman, Daniel G. "Irving's Use of American Folklore in 'The Legend of Sleepy Hollow.'" *PMLA,* 68 (June 1953), 425–435.

In a bibliography you give page numbers for the entire article.

Sample bibliographic entries for articles in popular publications

1. A weekly magazine.

> Rogoff, Gordon. "The Mere Human Props of Eugene O'Neill."
> *Saturday Review,* 28 May 1977, pp. 38–39.

2. A monthly magazine.

> Malone, Michael. "Books in Brief." *Harper's,* June 1977, pp.
> 82–84.

3. A book review in a weekly magazine.

> Seavey, Ormond. "Adventures and True Believers." Rev. of
> *Prophetic Waters: The River in Early American Life and
> Literature,* by John Seelye. *The Nation,* 11 June 1977,
> pp. 727–729.

4. An article in a newspaper.

> McLellan, Joseph. "'Il Trovatore' at Wolf Trap: Warming the
> Wind." *The Washington Post,* 8 June 1977, Sec. B, p.
> 7, col. 3.

SAMPLE RESEARCH PAPER

THE FORSAKEN SISTER

Roderick's Failure to Rescue Madeline

in Edgar Allan Poe's "The Fall of the House of Usher"

Perhaps the most obviously strange aspect of Edgar Allan
Poe's "The Fall of the House of Usher" is the setting. The bleak
landscape, dim tarn, crumbling mansion, and miasmic
atmosphere are nightmarish and inexplicable. They defy norms.
But equally strange is Roderick's behavior toward his sister,

Madeline. He claims to love her, and he grieves when she "dies."
But when he hears her trying to escape from her tomb, he
merely listens and waits. Why doesn't he rescue her?

The critical interpretations of the story are often as bizarre
as the story. They range from incest, to vampirism, to madness.[1]
But the interpretation that most meaningfully accounts for
Roderick's treatment of his sister is the symbolic. This view
holds that the story is symbolic of one person's deeply troubled
mind. Richard Wilbur, for example, contends that the "typical Poe
story occurs <u>within</u> the mind of a poet; and its characters are
not independent personalities, but allegorical figures
representing the warring principles of the poet's divided
nature."[2] "The Fall of the House of Usher," he says, is a "journey
into the depths of the self . . . a dream of the narrator's, in
which he leaves behind him the waking, physical world and
journeys inward toward his <u>moi intérieur,</u> toward his inner and
spiritual self. That inner and spiritual self is Roderick Usher."[3]
Roderick and Madeline, then, are symbolic of states of mind.
Daniel Hoffman agrees with Wilbur and sees the story as "a
terrifying tale of the protagonist's journey into the darkest, most
hidden regions of himself."[4] Hoffman argues that the story is the
narrator's dream.[5]

Edward H. Davidson offers a lucid explanation of what this
dream may represent. Like Wilbur and Hoffman, Davidson sees
the tale as an allegory of one person's mental disintegration. And
like them he sees the disintegration as caused by two warring
sides of the same mind. Roderick, he says, "represents the mind
or intellectual aspect" of the person. Madeline represents "the
sensual or physical side" of this same person.[6] Roderick "suffers
from the diseased mind which has too long abstracted itself from
physical reality; in fact, the physical world, and even the
physical side of himself, fills him with such repugnance that he
can maintain his unique world or self of the mind only by
destroying his twin sister or physical side of himself."[7] He tries
to bury her "in a place as far remote as possible from the place
of aesthetic delight wherein the mind of Roderick lives."[8] But he
cannot kill her, and she returns to kill both mind and body.[9] The
collapse of the house represents the collapse of "the total being
of this complex body-mind relation which Poe had studied in the
symbolic guise of a brother and sister relationship."[10]

Davidson does not discuss the story specifically, but a careful examination of it supports his theory. Not only does the story have, as Hoffman says, "the fixated, tableau-like rigidity, the inexorability, of a dream,"[11] but Poe hints that the story might be a dream. The narrator looks upon the house for the first time as if he were experiencing "the after-dream of the reveller upon opium."[12] As he examines the atmosphere enveloping the house, he tries to shake off from his spirit "what must have been a dream" (p. 400). For several days after he first sees Madeline, the narrator listens to Roderick's "wild improvisations" on the guitar "as if in a dream" (p. 404). And the climax of the story occurs in the middle of the night during a tempestuous storm, when the narrator cannot sleep and when his "fancy" becomes increasingly "excited" (p. 414).

As a "dream," the story projects psychological phenomena; the characters, setting, and events represent aspects of the mind. One key detail that supports this interpretation is "The Haunted Palace," the poem that Roderick sings to the narrator during a moment of "the highest artificial excitement" and that represents "the tottering of his [Roderick's] lofty reason upon her throne" (p. 406). "The Haunted Palace," as Wilbur points out, is the allegory of a man who goes mad. It represents two states of mind.[13] In the first half of the poem, the palace is described as a "head" inhabited by the "monarch," "Thought." It is topped by "banners yellow, glorious, golden" (hair). It has "two luminous windows" (eyes). Out of its "fair palace door" (mouth) come sounds (speech) that represent the "beauty," "wit," and "wisdom" (artistic productions, sane and noble ideas) of the "king." But all changes in the second half, when "evil things" assail the "monarch's high estate." The windows become "red." Inside, "vast forms" move "fantastically/To a discordant melody," and out of the "pale door" rushes "a hideous throng" that "laugh—but smile no more" (pp. 406–407).

A comparison of this allegorical house with the narrator's description of the Usher mansion, Wilbur says, leads to the realization that the Usher mansion "is, in allegorical fact, the physical body of Roderick Usher, and its dim interior is, in fact, Roderick Usher's visionary mind."[14] Details from the story support this interpretation. When the narrator sees the mansion for the first time, he describes it as having "vacant eye-like windows" (pp. 397–398), which make the mansion look like a head. He also thinks that "a mere different arrangement of the particulars of the scene, of the details of the picture, would be sufficient to modify, or perhaps to annihilate its capacity for sorrowful impression" (p. 398), as if the house has the flexible quality of the mind, the capacity for rearrangement and thus for sounder mental health. The narrator then says that the house is indeed symbolical; local peasants see it as an equivalent to the family. And the interior of the house, with its "many dark and intricate passages," its "feeble gleams of encrimsoned light," its rooms containing dark angles and recesses (pp. 400–401), resembles the complexity and mysteriousness of the mind.

The most important psychological phenomenon represented by the story is a mind at war with itself. Madeline is Roderick's twin, his mirror image: "her figure, her air, her features—all, in their very minutest development were those— were identically . . . those of the Roderick Usher who sat beside me" (p. 404). As such, she seems to represent one aspect of the mind contained within the house, an aspect that Roderick wants to suppress and destroy. But what does she represent?

An analysis of Roderick supports Davidson's claim that within the symbolic "house," two forces are at war. The character "Roderick" represents a desire to retreat from reality, whereas the character "Madeline" represents those qualities that make up reality—the physical, the sensuous, the bodily. Roderick's disease, for example, manifests itself as an extreme aversion to sensuous experiences—tasting, touching, smelling, seeing, hearing; that is, to all the ways the mind (through the body) receives and reacts to the physical world (p. 403). It is as if the intellect is retreating from the body. Roderick seems, furthermore, to have a morbid fear of the physical, especially as it is embodied by the house. He confesses to a conflict between his "spirit" and "the physique of the gray walls and turrets, and of the dim tarn into which they all looked down" (p. 408). His artistic products are further evidence of his escape from the physical world, from reality. Rather than paint real scenes, Roderick paints ideas, "pure abstractions," and "phantasmagoric conceptions" (p. 405). Rather than sing about real people and situations, he composes songs that are "fantastic," "fervid," "wild fantasies," and "artificial" (p. 406).

Roderick's apparently innate preference for the ideal over the real has led him to a practice that is the probable cause of his disease. He has increasingly isolated himself from the world outside his mind. The narrator traces the beginning of this process to Roderick's childhood, when his "reserve had been always excessive and habitual." Now the process is complete, for the narrator is his "best and indeed his only personal friend" (p. 398). But the disease represents a further extension of Roderick's isolation from the exterior world. Roderick has reached the point where he wants to isolate himself from everything physical, and that means especially from his body. The result is that Roderick's body, although still whole, is near the point of disintegration, a fact symbolized by the "barely perceptible fissure" that goes from top to bottom of the mansion (p. 400).

A logical extension of Roderick's tendency toward isolation is his obsession with death, the ultimate alienation from reality. When he plays his guitar and sings, he improvises dirges, most memorable of which is "a certain singular perversion and amplification of the wild air of the last waltz of Von Weber" (p. 405), a piece of music that Von Weber was reputed to have composed on his deathbed.[15] When among his books, Roderick's "chief delight" is perusing a "rare and curious" book detailing the last rites for the dead (p. 409). His most memorable painting seems to represent total and final isolation. It is of a "vault or tunnel" at "an exceeding depth" with "no outlet" and no natural sources of light (pp. 405–406).

Roderick's treatment of Madeline, the nature of her disease, and her subsequent behavior seem to indicate that she represents the physical, bodily world from which he is trying to escape. Her disease links her directly to the bodily, for it consists of "a gradual wasting away of the person" (p. 404). And after her first appearance, Roderick's own bodily strength diminishes: "a far more than ordinary wanness had overspread the emaciated fingers through which trickled many passionate tears" (p. 404). After he announces her "death," Roderick buries her in a vault that corresponds not only to the vault in his painting but to the oppressive atmosphere surrounding the Usher mansion. It is "small, damp, and entirely without means of admission for light." It lies at a "great depth." It seems impregnable and inescapable because of its "massive iron" door and archway "sheathed with copper." Its oxygenless "oppressive atmosphere"

half smothers the torches so that the light is lurid and dim
(p. 409).

All of these details suggest Roderick's obsessive, final
attempt to isolate his bodily self, to separate it from his
intellectual self. He even carries the entombment process further
by putting Madeline in a casket, screwing down the lid, and
locking the iron door. But one detail suggests that he will fail.
Even though Madeline seems "dead," she retains a surprising
physical vitality. She displays "the mockery of a faint blush upon
the bosom and the face, and [a] suspiciously lingering smile
upon the lip" (p. 410). When she finally emerges from her tomb,
her incredible physical strength is but a final detail linking her
to the physical and the bodily. Her resurrection seems to show
that repressing the physical side of the self results inevitably
in its overwhelming and powerful reassertion at a later
time.

Throughout the story, Roderick is pitiable. He seems to
recognize that he is in deep trouble. As a last attempt to help
himself, he reaches out to his only remaining contact with the
outside world, the narrator. He also seems to recognize the
importance of physical health and the tie of normal sensuous
experience to mental health. He loves Madeline, and in the first
half of "The Haunted Palace," he describes a healthy balance
between the sensuous and the intellectual. But by the time we see
him, he has carried the process of isolation too far to stop it.
Against his better judgment, he acts out allegorically the final
severing of mind and body. He buries Madeline, believing that
she—the body—is finally dead. When he realizes that she is still
alive, he refuses to rescue her because he wants her dead. His
mistake from the beginning was to think that the mind can
operate independently from the body, the intellectual from the
physical, the ideal from the real. In the end, he pays for his
mistake with his sanity and his life.

NOTES

[1]D. H. Lawrence in Studies in Classic American Literature
(New York: Penguin, 1977), pp. 84–85, and Leo Spitzer, "A
Reinterpretation of 'The Fall of the House of Usher,'" in
Twentieth-Century Interpretations of "The Fall of the House of

Usher," ed. Thomas Woodson (Englewood Cliffs, N. J.: Prentice-Hall, 1969), p. 58, argue for the incest theory. A supporter of the vampire theory is Lyle H. Kendall, "The Vampire Motif in 'The Fall of the House of Usher,'" in Twentieth-Century Interpretations of "The Fall of the House of Usher," ed. Thomas Woodson (Englewood Cliffs, N. J.: Prentice-Hall, 1969), pp. 99–104. John S. Hill in "The Dual Hallucination in 'The Fall of the House of Usher,'" Southwest Review, 48 (Autumn 1963), 396–402, and I. M. Walker in "The 'Legitimate Sources' of Terror in 'The Fall of the House of Usher,'" Modern Language Review, 61 (October 1966), 585–592, claim that Madeline really dies and that both the narrator and Roderick go mad and hallucinate her resurrection.

[2]"The House of Poe," in The Recognition of Edgar Allan Poe: Selected Criticism since 1829, ed. Eric W. Carlson (Ann Arbor: Univ. of Michigan Press, 1966), pp. 274–275.

[3]Wilbur, p. 265.

[4]Poe Poe Poe Poe Poe Poe (Garden City, N. Y.: Doubleday, 1972), p. 302.

[5]Hoffman, p. 307.

[6]Poe: A Critical Study (Cambridge, Mass.: Harvard Univ. Press, 1957), p. 197.

[7]Davidson, p. 197.

[8]Davidson, p. 197.

[9]Davidson, p. 198.

[10]Davidson, p. 198.

[11]Hoffman, p. 307.

[12]"The Fall of the House of Usher," in Collected Works of Edgar Allan Poe, ed. Thomas Ollive Mabbott (Cambridge, Mass.: Harvard Univ. Press, 1978), II, 397. Further references to the

story will be to this edition and will appear in parentheses in the text.

[13]Wilbur, p. 263.

[14]Wilbur, p. 264.

[15]Collected Works of Edgar Allan Poe, p. 405, n. 9.

BIBLIOGRAPHY OF WORKS CONSULTED

Abel, Darrel. "A Key to the House of Usher." In Twentieth-
    Century Interpretations of "The Fall of the House of Usher."
    Ed. Thomas Woodson. Englewood Cliffs, N. J.: Prentice-Hall,
    1969, pp. 43–55.
Davidson, Edward H. Poe: A Critical Study. Cambridge, Mass.:
    Harvard Univ. Press, 1957.
Hill, John S. "The Dual Hallucination in 'The Fall of the House of
    Usher.'" Southwest Review, 48 (Autumn 1963), 396–402.
Hoffman, Daniel. Poe Poe Poe Poe Poe Poe. Garden City, N. Y.:
    Doubleday, 1972.
Kendall, Lyle H. "The Vampire Motif in 'The Fall of the House of
    Usher.'" In Twentieth-Century Interpretations of "The Fall of
    the House of Usher." Ed. Thomas Woodson. Englewood Cliffs,
    N. J.: Prentice-Hall, 1969, pp. 99–104.
Lawrence, D. H. Studies in Classic American Literature. New
    York: Penguin, 1977.
Poe, Edgar Allan. "The Fall of the House of Usher." In Collected
    Works of Edgar Allan Poe. Ed. Thomas Ollive Mabbott. Vol. II.
    Cambridge, Mass.: Harvard Univ. Press, 1978, pp. 392–422.
Spitzer, Leo. "A Reinterpretation of 'The Fall of the House of
    Usher.'" In Twentieth-Century Interpretations of "The Fall of
    the House of Usher." Ed. Thomas Woodson. Englewood Cliffs,
    N. J.: Prentice-Hall, 1969, pp. 56–70.
Stein, William Bysshe. "The Twin Motif in 'The Fall of the House
    of Usher.'" Modern Language Notes, 75 (February 1960),
    109–111.
Walker, I. M. "The 'Legitimate Sources' of Terror in 'The Fall of
    the House of Usher.'" Modern Language Review, 61 (October
    1966), 585–592.
Wilbur, Richard. "The House of Poe." In The Recognition of Edgar

<u>Allan Poe: Selected Criticism since 1829.</u> Ed. Eric W. Carlson.
Ann Arbor: Univ. of Michigan Press, 1966, pp. 255–277.

Analysis of the sample research paper

Notice the way this paper begins. The writer raises a question
about the story. She states that question in the first paragraph, or
introduction. In the rest of the essay, the writer argues in favor of
a certain answer to the question. The paper, in short, is an essay. It
has a narrowly focused topic, a thesis, and a structure like other
essays about literature. Its purpose is to enlighten and convince the
reader. It is a "research paper" because it uses research as a tool to
solve a problem, but it is nonetheless an essay.

In the second paragraph, the writer introduces the research
part of the essay. After explaining that she surveyed literary criticism of the story, the writer passes quickly over interpretations that
are not helpful to the thesis and lights upon one that is—the symbolic interpretation. The writer then accurately and fully explains
that approach in the second and third paragraphs. These paragraphs contain the bulk of the references to research material and
thus almost all of the footnotes. But the critical theory does not in
itself answer the writer's question. It merely shows how the question might be answered. The writer proceeds to answer the question in the rest of the essay by analyzing the story in detail, using
the critical theory as a guide. The transition sentence of the fourth
paragraph ("Davidson does not discuss the story specifically, but a
careful examination of it supports his theory") signals the beginning of this part of the essay. In the last paragraph of the essay, the
writer answers the question and, in so doing, states her thesis. The
"Notes" page provides documentation for specific citations. The
bibliography gives a convenient list of sources cited and sources
consulted.

Not all research essays will be structured like this one, but
this essay has a simple and functional organization that you might
find useful when structuring your own research essays. First, it
states the problem (question) in an introductory paragraph. Second, it surveys the pertinent literary criticism and fully explains
what the writer believes is the most relevant approach. Third, it
examines the work in light of this approach. This third part of the
essay is the longest and most important. It represents the writer's

use of the critical approach to solve the problem. In this section, you might continue to draw upon secondary sources, as this essay does (see notes 13, 14, and 15). But otherwise, you are on your own. Fourth, in a concluding paragraph, the writer states a solution to the problem, an answer to the question. This answer is the essay's thesis.

FREQUENTLY USED ABBREVIATIONS

When you read essays and books about literature, you will often run into abbreviations. When you write your own essays, you may want to resort to some of the more well-known and space-saving of these abbreviations. Here, then, is a list of them. Many pertain to essays that use secondary sources.

c., ca.	*circa,* "about" (usually used with dates when the exact date is not certain—for example, ca. 1594)
cf.	*confer,* "compare" (not the equivalent of "see")
ch., chs.	chapter, chapters
d.	died
ed., eds.	edited by, editor, editors
esp.	especially
e.g.	*exempli gratia,* "for example"
et al.	*et alii,* "and others"
etc.	*et cetera,* "and so forth"
f., ff.	and the following (pages)
ibid.	*ibidem,* "in the same place" (but avoid using *ibid.* in your own research papers)
i.e.	*id est,* "that is"
l., ll.	line, lines
ms., mss.	manuscript, manuscripts
N.B.	*nota bene,* "note well"
p., pp.	page, pages
q.v.	*quod vide,* "which see"
viz.	*videlicet,* "namely"
vol., vols.	volume, volumes

10

Mechanical matters relating to essays about literature

THIS CHAPTER CONTAINS rules or guidelines about matters that are mainly "mechanical"—that is, they involve procedures that are reasonably clear and easy to follow consistently. The bulk of the material in this chapter pertains to rules of usage. *Usage* here means the way educated speakers and writers in the United States use English on formal and semiformal occasions. A standard handbook of usage is *The Harbrace College Handbook*. The rules covered here are common to essays about literature.

HOW TO HANDLE QUOTATIONS

Quotations are a frequent and essential part of most essays about literature. They serve two key purposes: they help to exemplify generalizations (points) that the writer of the essay makes, and they represent directly the felicitous or characteristic language of a source.

1. Introduce your quotations.

   a. For primary sources, identify the author, the work, and the context of quotations.

      WRONG: The woman tells her lover that the world "isn't ours anymore."

RIGHT: Near the climax of the lovers' conversation in Hemingway's "Hills Like White Elephants," the woman tells the man that the world "isn't ours anymore."

The reason for this rule is that quotations take on significance because of what surrounds them. Often, as in the above example, the quotation is meaningless unless the reader knows where it occurs in the story.

b. Introduce quotations from secondary sources by giving the author's name or claim to authority:

WRONG: "A fully articulated pastoral idea of America did not emerge until the end of the eighteenth century."

RIGHT: Leo Marx claims that a "fully articulated pastoral idea of America did not emerge until the end of the eighteenth century."

RIGHT: A prominent American critic claims that a "fully articulated. . . ."

There are several reasons for this rule. One is that giving the critic's name or claim to authority clearly distinguishes your ideas from the other writer's. Quotation marks help to make this distinction, of course, but introducing the quote by author makes the distinction emphatic. A second reason is that when readers see quotation marks, they are naturally curious about who said the quoted passage. And, as they read your essay, they may want to keep track of the different approaches of the critics you are using. A third reason is that by giving the author's name, you distinguish between secondary and primary sources. The distinction may not be clear just from the quotation itself. A final reason is that it is a matter of courtesy to give credit in your text to the words and ideas of other people. It is as if you are standing before an audience making a speech, and for support of your argument you bring forth real people to speak on your behalf. In such a situation, you would always introduce them by name to your audience before they spoke. You are not just giving them credit; you are, in a way, thanking them.

c. Introduce quotations with the correct mark of punctuation. Use a comma for brief, informal, grammatically incomplete introductions.

WRONG: Prufrock thinks ''I am no prophet—and here's no great matter.''

RIGHT: Prufrock thinks, ''I am no prophet—and here's no great matter.''

Use a colon to separate your own grammatically complete introductions or statements (complete sentences) from quotations.

WRONG: Edith Hamilton describes Hera perfectly, ''She was the protector of marriage, and married women were her peculiar care. There is very little that is attractive in the portrait the poets draw of her.''

RIGHT: Edith Hamilton describes Hera perfectly: ''She was the protector. . . .''

The rules of usage here are to a degree arbitrary. But their main function is to separate your thoughts from those of the quotation—that is, to eliminate ambiguity. Thus, the first examples above mean two different things. Without the comma, the reader might see the whole sentence as one complete thought: "Prufrock thinks [that] "I am no prophet—and here's no great matter." With the comma, the reader sees that "Prufrock thinks" is merely the introduction to the quotation; the quotation is the complete thought.

2. Integrate quotations into your own sentences.

EXAMPLE: Because of this increasing darkness, Brown cannot be quite sure of what he does or hears. The devil's walking stick, for example, seems to turn into a snake, but this may be ''an ocular deception, assisted by the uncertain light'' (p. 76). He thinks he hears the voices of Deacon Gookin and the minister, but ''owing doubtless to the depth of the gloom of

that particular spot, neither the travellers nor their steeds
were visible" (p. 81).

Once you have properly introduced your source, you may want
to integrate short quotations from it into your own sentences,
as in the above example. The quotations, then, become part of
your own thoughts rather than thoughts totally separate from
yours. This technique is most useful when you want to summarize a source concisely and yet retain something of the language and authenticity of the source. If you use this method,
you should obey several rules.

a. Keep all tenses the same. Change the tenses in the quotation
to correspond to your tenses, putting your words in brackets. When writing about fictional events, for example,
change quoted verbs to the present tense.

WRONG: While the legislators cringe at the sudden darkness,
"all eyes were turned to Abraham Davenport."

RIGHT: While the legislators cringe at the sudden darkness,
"all eyes [turn] to Abraham Davenport."

b. Make sure that sentences are complete.

WRONG: Yeats asks if "before the indifferent beak." [Incom-
plete sentence; it makes no sense.]

RIGHT: Yeats asks if Leda "put on [the swan's] knowledge"
before his "indifferent beak could let her drop."

c. Clarify pronouns that have no clear antecedents.

WRONG: Captain Wentworth says, "It had been my doing—
solely mine. She would not have been obstinate if I had not
been weak." [This quotation is wrongly handled if the ante-
cedent of "she" is unclear.]

RIGHT: Captain Wentworth says, "It had been my doing—
solely mine. [Louisa] would not have been obstinate if I had
not been weak."

d. Make sure that subject and verb agree.

> WRONG: Wilfred Owen says that the only prayer said for those who die in battle is war's noise, which "patter out their hasty orisons." [Subject: "noise"; verb: "patter." The subject is singular, the verb plural.]

> RIGHT: Wilfred Owen says that the only prayer said for those who die in battle is the "rapid rattle" of guns, which "patter out their hasty orisons." [Subject: "guns"; verb: "patter." Both subject and verb are now plural.]

In short, when you integrate a quotation into your sentence, it becomes a grammatical part of the sentence. You need to make the whole sentence, including the quotation, conform to all the rules of usage that you would normally obey when writing any other sentence. See Section 4 below for methods of altering (interpolating) quotations to align them with your sentences.

3. <u>Quote accurately.</u> Copy exactly what the author has written.

4. <u>Make editorial changes in quotations correctly.</u> You may legitimately change the quotation in three ways:

   a. By using an *ellipsis*. The ellipsis (three spaced periods) indicates material omitted. You may want to do this for brevity's sake.

   > EXAMPLE: As one critic says, "Oedipus is guilty for two reasons: because of the deeds he actually committed . . . and because of his *desire* to commit them."

   When you omit the last part of a sentence, the ellipsis precedes the period. Thus all four periods are spaced.

   > EXAMPLE: "Treat your wife badly . . . . Is this what you believe in?"

When you omit material *between* complete sentences, the ellipsis follows the period of the preceding sentence.

EXAMPLE: "Well, and how will you make love to me? Come, I long to have you begin. . . . You must tell me how."

The first period is not spaced (because it indicates the end of the sentence that begins with "Come"), but the remaining three are (because they represent the omitted material).

b. By using *brackets*. Brackets indicate editorial changes that *you,* not the author, make to clarify the quotation or to make it fit the grammatical structure of your sentence. Do not use parentheses to indicate such changes; otherwise, your reader will see them as part of the original quote.

WRONG: Alceste says that "sins which cause the blood to freeze/Look innocent beside (Célimène's) treacheries."

RIGHT: "She looked carefully for the place where [Elizabeth] had entered the garden."

RIGHT: Flaubert says that "she [has] an excess of energy."

If you are typing your essay, either draw the brackets in by hand, or type them in with the slant-line key and the underscore key.

c. By adjusting the *initial letter and final mark of punctuation* to fit the grammatical requirements of your sentence.

EXAMPLE: As Gabriel watches the snowflakes "falling obliquely against the lamplight," he realizes that "the time [has] come for him to set out on his journey westward."

This example draws on two sentences from Joyce's "The Dead": (1) "He watched sleepily the flakes silver and dark, falling obliquely against the lamplight." (2) "The time had come for him to set out on his journey westward." The example substitutes a comma for the period in the first sentence and reduces the initial letter of the second sentence to lower case.

5. <u>Indent long quotations.</u> A "long" quotation is more than three lines of poetry or more than fifty words of prose. Usually, your introduction to a long quotation will be a complete sentence. Conclude your sentence, then, with a *colon* (not a comma or a period). Double-space from your text. Indent ten spaces from the left margin. *Do not* put indented quotations in quotation marks. Single-space the quote.

> EXAMPLE: The duke is chagrined that his own name and presence were not the sole sources of her joy:

She had

> A heart—how shall I say?—too soon made glad,
> Too easily impressed; she liked whate'er
> She looked on, and her looks went everywhere.
> Sir, 'twas all one! My favour at her breast,
> The dropping of the daylight in the West,
> The bough of cherries some officious fool
> Broke in the orchard for her, the white mule
> She rode with round the terrace—all and each
> Would draw from her alike the approving speech,
> Or blush, at least.

As in this example, keep the first words of a quoted poem exactly where they come in the line. For prose quotations, do not indicate paragraph indentations unless you are quoting more than one paragraph.

6. <u>Punctuate quotations correctly.</u>

a. Use *double quotation marks* (" ") for quotations. For quotations within quotations, use double quotation marks for the main quote and single quotation marks (the apostrophe mark on the typewriter) for the inner quote.

> EXAMPLE: After his interview with Hester, Dimmesdale sinks into self-doubt: "'Have I then sold myself,' thought the min-

ister, 'to the fiend whom, if men say true, this yellow-starched and velveted old hag has chosen for her prince and master!'"

b. Always put *periods and commas* inside quotation marks.

EXAMPLE: After performing her "duties to God," as she called them, she was ready for her "duty to man."

c. Always put *colons and semicolons* outside of quotation marks.

EXAMPLE: She had the "exquisite pleasure of art"; her husband had only envy and hatred.

d. Put *other marks of punctuation* (question marks, dashes, exclamation points) inside quotation marks when they are part of the quoted material, outside when they are not.

EXAMPLE: As one critic put it, "Could the Pearl Poet really be the author of *Sir Gawain and the Green Knight?*"

EXAMPLE: But can it be, as one critic claims, that "the Pearl Poet really [is] the author of *Sir Gawain and the Green Knight*"?

e. *When quoting poetry,* indicate line divisions with slash marks. This rule *does not* apply when you indent your poetry quotation. (You may prefer to indent even short quotations from poetry. Doing so preserves the visual integrity of the poem.)

ACCEPTABLE: Hopkins describes God's grandeur as gathering "to a greatness, like the ooze of oil/Crushed."

BETTER: Hopkins describes God's grandeur as gathering

> to a greatness, like the ooze of oil
> Crushed.

f. For punctuating the *parenthetical page references* that often follow quotations, see "Making subsequent references to primary sources," pp. 126–127, Chapter 9. The sample essays in Chapter 12 also provide extensive examples of how these references are handled.

OTHER RULES OF USAGE

Essays about literature obey the same mechanical conventions as other essays, but several rules deserve special mention.

1. <u>Tense.</u> Describe fictional events, whether in drama, poetry, or prose fiction, in the present tense.

2. <u>Authors' names.</u> Use either the full name (Charles Dickens) or the last name (Dickens). Some exceptions are Lord Byron, Mrs. Browning, and Dr. Johnson.

3. Titles.

   a. Capitalize the first letter of all words in a title except articles, prepositions, and conjunctions.

      EXAMPLE: "How I Won the World but Lost My Soul to the Devil's Wiles"

   b. Use quotation marks when you give the titles of short stories, essays, short poems, songs, chapter titles, articles, and unpublished works such as dissertations and Master's theses.

   c. Underline (put in italics) the titles of books, plays, long poems, pamphlets, periodicals, movies, works of art, works of music. An exception is books of the Bible and the Bible itself; both are capitalized but not underlined.

   d. Do not underline or put in quotation marks the titles of your own essays.

   e. Many instructors prefer that your essay titles include full names of authors and works.

WRONG: The Four Stages of Knowledge in Twain's *Huck Finn*

RIGHT: The Four Stages of Knowledge in Mark Twain's *The Adventures of Huckleberry Finn*

THE PHYSICAL APPEARANCE OF YOUR ESSAY

The appearance of your essay affects your argument. The appearance projects you and your attitudes. The better your essay looks, the more favorably your reader will think of your argument. Your overall goal should be to make your essay pleasant to see, pleasant to hold, and easy to read. Although your instructor may have specific preferences, the following are standard guidelines.

1. Typewritten and handwritten essays. Some instructors may prefer that you type all your work, but usually you may either type or handwrite college essays. Whether you handwrite or type your essay, use only one side of the page. For handwritten essays, use black or blue ink (which, unlike pencil, won't smear or rub off). Use lined paper. Write on every other line if the lines are closely spaced. Above all, write legibly. If you type your essays, double-space. Use a good typewriter ribbon. Clean your type.

2. Paper. Use standard-size paper ($8\frac{1}{2} \times 11$ inches), not legal-pad size or notepad size. Use a sturdy weight of paper. Never use onionskin paper except for carbon copies. Avoid "erasable" paper; it does not take corrections in ink well and it is sticky. In a warm place it is very unpleasant to handle. Don't hand in essays written on pages that have been ripped out of a spiral-bound notebook.

3. Pagination. Number pages consecutively, including footnote and bibliography pages. Put the page number at the center or upper right-hand corner of each page. If you think that a page might get misplaced, put your last name before each page number.

4. Margins. For typewritten essays, leave 1- to $1\frac{1}{2}$-inch margins at top, bottom, and sides. This gives the page a "frame" and a place for the instructor's comments. For handwritten essays, leave margins at top, bottom, and left side.

5. First page. Put your name, course title, date, and assignment in the upper right-hand corner. Double-space and center your title. Double-space again and begin your essay. Title pages are usually not necessary, but if your instructor expects a title page, check with him or her for its content and form, or consult a rhetoric handbook.

6. Corrections. You may write corrections on final copies of essays if the corrections are few and fairly inconspicuous. In typed essays, erase incorrect letters and write or type in the correct letters. Draw a vertical line through an incorrect letter in a handwritten essay and write the correct letter just above the line. Separate run-together words with vertical lines (for example, made/a/mistake). To delete words, phrases, and clauses, draw a single horizontal line through them. Add words, phrases, and clauses by writing them in above the line. Use a caret ($\wedge$) to show where inserted material should go.

7. Putting the essay pages together. Use a paper clip to combine the pages of your essay unless your instructor specifies some other method.

8. Copies. Make a photocopy or carbon copy of your essay. If your instructor should lose your essay, you can immediately present him or her with the copy of your finished essay. Or if your instructor keeps your essay indefinitely, you will have the copy for your files. When you turn in the essay the first time, however, turn in the original, not the copy.

9. To fold or not to fold. Leave your essay unfolded unless your instructor specifies otherwise.

11

How to take essay tests

S O FAR, THIS BOOK has dealt with essays written outside the classroom. "Tests" and "examinations," however, are work that you do in class, usually within a given time. When your instructor tests you, he or she wants to know two things: how familiar you are with the course material (the literature, the instructor's lectures, the secondary material you may be required to read) and how creatively you can think about this material. Tests fall into two categories, factual and essay. Sometimes the instructor may include questions, or assignments, from both categories on the same test.

Factual tests ask you to account for, explain, and identify details about the course material. Essay tests ask you to state your ideas about literary works and to support those ideas with facts. Some essay tests call for short, one-paragraph essays; some call for long essays. But the same methods for writing out-of-class essays apply to test essays, short or long. Your test essays are arguments. They should have a thesis. They should try to convince an audience of the validity of that thesis. They should use sound logic and apt illustrations. Most of all, because of time limits, they need good organization. Perhaps the most important general consideration to keep in mind is that your grade will depend on how well you *perform* on a particular assignment, not simply on how much you know. You may know the material very well, but if you do not perform well, your grade will not reflect the abundance or quality of your knowledge. The following guidelines should help you perform well.

GUIDELINES FOR TAKING AN ESSAY TEST

1. <u>Prepare thoroughly.</u>

    a. First, learn the facts of the material—of the work or works on which you are being tested. Know who the characters are, what they do and what happens to them, the specifics of setting. When you are taking the test, you should know the details so well that they emerge from your memory almost automatically. This subliminal knowledge saves your creative energy for dealing with the interpretive problems the instructor gives you. If you have to dredge up facts from your memory slowly, you waste valuable test time.

    b. Systematically review the key problems or subjects relevant to the works, literary periods, or genres covered by the test. A good way to do this is to ask questions, as you would for finding essay topics. Here, however, you try to cover all the important questions. A knowledge of the elements of literature is especially useful for systematic questioning. How does the author handle setting? characterization? structure? theme? point of view? and so forth.

    c. Review class notes. But do so *in conjunction with* a review of the literary works. Reviewing your notes on the instructor's class comments should help to pinpoint important aspects of the works and should help you anticipate test questions. Remember, however, that memorizing class notes is no substitute for reviewing the works themselves. The two should be done together.

2. <u>Understand the assignment.</u> When you get the test, read all of the assignments carefully before you begin writing. If you do not understand some of them, ask the instructor to explain more fully. Sometimes instructors unintentionally write ambiguous

assignments. You have a right to know exactly what you are supposed to do.

3. Plan your answer.

   a. Take a few minutes to make a short, topical outline. One advantage of making an outline is that it frees you from worrying about being relevant or complete. Instead, you can devote your whole attention to a creative development of each main point. If you have fifty minutes to write an essay, ten minutes making an outline will be time well spent.

   b. Exclude irrelevant topics.

   c. Arrange the remaining topics in a logical order. It may be that descending order of importance will be the most practical order for your answer. That way, if you run out of time, you will still have covered your most important points.

4. Address yourself to the assignment. Anything irrelevant to the assignment wastes words and time.

5. Give a direct response to the assignment. One or two sentences somewhere in your answer should do the job. This way the instructor will know that you have kept the assignment in mind and that you have tried to deal with it. Your direct response to the assignment is the thesis of your essay and therefore usually should come near the beginning or end of your essay. Note the following example:

> *Assignment:* Huck tricks Jim into believing that he dreamed they were separated in the fog. But Jim finally sees the trick for what it is. What does Huck learn from Jim's reaction?

> *Direct response:* Huck learns that Jim has feelings and dignity just as white people do.

The complete answer, of course, would explain and illustrate this point fully, but the direct response connects the whole answer firmly to the assignment. Without a direct response, your answer may seem irrelevant.

6. <u>Write in a clear, simple, and correct style.</u> The limited time and the pressure of the occasion make some mechanical slips likely, but you should be able to avoid most of them. Be especially careful to avoid serious errors like sentence fragments, comma splices, ambiguous pronoun references, and subject/verb disagreement. If your handwriting is normally difficult to read, take care to make it legible.

7. <u>Develop your answer thoroughly.</u>

   a. Make generalizations that respond directly to the assignment. Often, these generalizations will serve as topic sentences for paragraphs.

   b. Offer specific details from the works that support and illustrate your generalizations.

   c. Represent the work or works adequately. The more thoroughly and aptly you relate the work to your generalizations (and thus to the assignment), the better your answer will be.

   d. Your answer is an argument. You must back up your points with evidence. Therefore, don't just tell your readers, show them.

8. <u>Be creative.</u> Some instructors want no more from you on a test than a perfect reproduction of what they have said in class. Studying for their tests, then, is simple. You just memorize what the instructor has said and paraphrase it on the test. The more perfect your reproduction, the better your grade. But other instructors want more, and they design their tests to get more. They want *your* thinking, not just their own. They want your creativity. But how can you be creative on tests? The answer is—think for yourself! Here are some ways to do so.

   a. Use the instructor's points but provide your own examples from the works. This shows the instructor that you are doing more than just memorizing lectures. It shows that you have thought through and applied the instructor's ideas on your own.

   b. Find your own points. Although instructors try to cover the most important aspects of a work, limited class time makes it impossible for them to cover every aspect, even all the important ones. There are usually plenty of other points to be made. Study the work yourself and come up with your own points. Read what others have said about the work, and discover points that way. You should not neglect the points made by the instructor when you write test answers, but you can display your own thinking by making other points as well.

c. Address yourself to controversies inherent in works of literature and take a stand. Often the instructor will discuss such controversies in class (like the controversy about the ending of *Huckleberry Finn,* discussed in Chapter 1). In addition, controversies about works become apparent when you read literary criticism on them. Understanding these controversies will sharpen your perception of the work. Showing your awareness of them and taking a stand on them will demonstrate your creative involvement with the work.

d. Disagree with the instructor. This is risky but certainly creative. If you are brave enough to do this, have plenty of facts and logic at hand. Be diplomatic. Some instructors invite disagreement and thus encourage a critical dialogue between themselves and their students.

e. Be detailed in your support and illustration of points. The more details you provide, the clearer your creative involvement becomes, especially if some of the details are those you have noticed on your own.

SAMPLE TEST ESSAYS

All of the following essays respond to the assignment below. The writers had about twenty minutes to write their essays.

> *ASSIGNMENT:* Many stories contain objects that take on symbolic value. These objects represent ideas that emerge from the characters and events in the stories. Explain the possible symbolic importance of the rocking horse in D. H. Lawrence's "The Rocking Horse Winner."

Essay 1

Paul seems desperately to want his mother to love him. He senses that somehow she disapproves of him, that he stands in her way of achieving happiness. He seeks solace in the rocking horse. She has told him that "luck" means having money, so he rides the horse to get money. He hopes that by giving his mother money, he can buy his way into her heart. But, unfortunately, when he gives her an enormous sum of money, she is even more unhappy than before. Paul returns to the rocking horse to get more money for her. He frantically rides the horse one last time. But although he wins the jackpot, he dies from overexcitement and exhaustion.

Analysis of essay 1

This is a mediocre essay because it does not directly address the assignment. It describes the action of the story accurately. It is clearly written. Its organization is easy to follow. It seems to have the assignment vaguely in mind. But nowhere does it say what the rocking horse symbolizes. The instructor can guess what the writer has in mind, but cannot know for sure. Possibly because of this lack of focus, the essay omits important details. The writer doesn't say, for example, how Paul uses the horse to win money. The instructor may wonder whether the writer has read the story carefully.

Essay 2

Paul's mother claims that she is "unlucky," and she explains to Paul that being unlucky means having no money. But the details of the story suggest that Paul's family does have money, because they live very well. The family has the trappings of wealth—a nurse, a large house, comfortable furnishings, and a gardener. The mother, then, isn't really poor but is obsessed with money. Her children sense this obsession. Most sensitive of all is Paul, who hears voices saying, "There must be more money." As a result, Paul sets out to win his mother's love by being "lucky." His means of achieving luck and thus his mother's love is the rocking horse. He finds that by riding the horse hard enough, he can predict winners of horse races. The rocking horse, then, symbolizes the love his mother has withheld from him. He even experiences something like the ecstasy of love when riding the horse to a winner. But his plan fails when his gift of 5,000 pounds only makes his mother's greed greater. He then becomes so desperate for love that he rides the rocking horse to his death.

Analysis of essay 2

This is a good essay. It not only accurately recounts details from the story but directly responds to the assignment, and it relates all the details cited from the story to that response. In other words, the details become "evidence." Because it deals directly with the assignment, it treats the story more specifically and thoroughly than does essay 1.

Essay 3

The rocking horse symbolizes many things in "The Rocking Horse Winner." Paul's mother complains that she has no money, and she tells Paul that to be "lucky" is to have money. Paul is very impressed by what she says and decides to prove to her that he is lucky. He wants also to stop the voices in the house that incessantly demand more money. He feels that the rocking horse can take him where luck is. And, sure enough, when he rides the rocking horse and it takes him "there," he can predict the winners of horse races and make a great deal of money. So one thing the rocking horse symbolizes is luck, which, in turn, means money.

But the rocking horse also seems to represent a second idea. Paul's uncle says after Paul dies that he is better off being dead than living in a world where he had to ride a rocking horse to find a winner. The implication is that Paul was using the rocking horse to get what his mother never gave him, her love. So the rocking horse also symbolizes Paul's need for love and his parents' failure to give him affection.

Finally, the rocking horse symbolizes success. When Paul rides the rocking horse far enough, it brings him financial success. But this success is only ironic, for it never brings him the "success" he desperately wants—

his mother's love—and in the end it brings him death. Lawrence seems to suggest that some kinds of success are better than others; it is better to be loved than to be rich.

Analysis of essay 3

This is an excellent answer. Like essay 2, the essay directly responds to the assignment, and it plausibly and logically connects details of the story to its points. But it is more detailed and creative than essay 2. The writer makes a strong case for the complexity of the rocking horse as symbol and, by so doing, uncovers the multiple meanings and richness of the story. Whereas essay 2 sees only one possible meaning of the rocking horse, essay 3 sees three, all of which the writer explains convincingly.

12

Sample essays about literature

HIS CHAPTER CONTAINS six sample essays. Two are about fiction, two about poetry, and two about drama. All literary essays, of course, are different; problems are different and writers have different methods of solving them. These essays, then, are not models to be slavishly imitated. But they do embody the main points of this book: that essays about literature are arguments, that their topics contain implicit questions, that their theses are answers to these questions, that they should convincingly support their theses, and that they should speak to a general audience of interested readers.

CONFLICT IN SHIRLEY JACKSON'S
"THE LOTTERY"

Shirley Jackson seems to want us to feel shocked and horrified at the conclusion of her chilling story "The Lottery." We see a group of human beings doing one of the worst deeds imaginable—cold-bloodedly murdering a defenseless person whom they all know and love. We wonder, Will the villagers ever stop doing such a terrible thing? The answer to this

This is the central question of the essay.

The next sentence indicates the writer's *method* of answering the question.

Topic sentence. This paragraph deals with the first half of the conflict.

Footnote reference to the primary source.

Subsequent references to the primary source.

A specific reference that is not a quotation but that needs a page citation.

Quotations introduced with a colon.

question seems to lie in the resolution of an important conflict—a conflict between the villagers' reluctance to participate in the lottery and their eagerness to participate.

Their reluctance to participate is evident from the beginning. The men standing around waiting are subdued: "Their jokes were quiet and they smiled rather than laughed."[1] The children, when called, come "reluctantly, having to be called four or five times" (p. 219). Once the black box is brought out, the villagers keep "their distance" from it (p. 219). The fact that people have made no attempt to repair the old black box suggests that when the box wears out, perhaps they will let the custom die. The ritual surrounding the lottery has also been neglected, so that only fragments are remembered and practiced (p. 220). Once Mr. Summers begins the formal proceedings, Mrs. Dunbar is uneasy that her sixteen-year-old boy might even be thought eligible to stand in for his father (p. 221). When Mr. Adams' name, the first name, is called, he and Mr. Summers grin at each other "humorlessly and nervously" (p. 222). Mrs. Delacroix says to Mrs. Summers: "Seems like there's no time at all between lotteries any more" (p. 222), as if the people find the lotteries unpleasant and put them out of mind as soon as they are over. She holds her breath as her husband goes forward to draw a name (p. 222). We learn that there is some restiveness outside the village over lotteries: "over in the north village they're talking of giving up the lottery"; "some places have already quit lotteries" (p. 222). The most obvious example of reluctance is Mrs. Hutchinson, who, as soon as her family is chosen, questions the fairness of the draw. She does not, it should be noted, question the fairness of lotteries, just of the particular draw:

An interpolation (put in brackets).

Transition sentence.

Topic sentence. This paragraph deals with the second half of the conflict mentioned in the last sentence of the first paragraph.

Topic sentence. The writer reminds readers of the essay's purpose by asking which side will win.

"You didn't give him [her husband] time enough to take any paper he wanted. I saw you. It wasn't fair" (p. 223). Her reluctance to participate grows, of course, and reaches its apex at the very end, just before her death.

Throughout the village, then, people are generally reluctant to participate in the lottery. But their attitude toward the lottery is ambivalent, for they seem eager to participate as well. This eagerness emerges early in the story. Some of the children are apparently the most eager. They are on the scene first. Bobby Martin has "already stuffed his pockets full of stones," and the other boys soon do likewise; some even make piles of stones (p. 219). Ironically, Mrs. Hutchinson is, at first, the most eager adult. She rushes disheveled to the square and tells Mrs. Delacroix that she "clean forgot what day it was" until she noticed her children were gone. Then "I remembered it was the twenty-seventh and came a-running" (p. 221). Mrs. Delacroix assures her that she is "in time" since "they're still talking away up there" (p. 221). Once the drawing begins, Mrs. Dunbar tells her son to "get ready to run tell Dad" (p. 223). Mrs. Delacroix picks up the largest stone she can find and tells Mrs. Dunbar, "Come on. . . . Hurry up" (p. 225). Mrs. Dunbar has stones in both hands and, "gasping for breath," claims that she "can't run at all"; she will have to catch up. The children already have stones, and someone gives little Davy Hutchinson a few. Old Man Warner says, "Come on, come on, everyone" as they all close in on Mrs. Hutchinson for the kill (p. 225).

Which of these two conflicting attitudes toward the lottery will become dominant? The villagers' reluctance to participate and the discontinuance of lotteries elsewhere suggests that lotteries may end here as well. But there is a weakness in the villagers' reluctance to participate. Their reluctance is selfishly motivated. No one objects to the lottery on behalf of someone else. Only the victim is critical of it. It is true that some people exhibit uneasiness when loved ones and children might be victims. Perhaps the villagers are moving, however slowly, toward the belief that human life is a good in itself and must not be wantonly destroyed. But not until then will they be able to abolish the lottery as a communal evil. In contrast, the villagers' eagerness to participate is very strong. The lottery, we learn, is irrational. Only Mr. Warner, the oldest of the villagers, has an inkling of why lotteries are held at all: "Lottery in June, corn be heavy soon" (p. 222). No one else remembers why they have lotteries. What everyone does remember is how to kill. The murder, which for the reader is the most horrible part of the lottery, is for the villagers the most important part, the part they take most for granted. So eager are they to participate that they risk being chosen themselves just to be there.

Topic sentence.

Throughout the essay, the writer builds toward a conclusion while at the same time revealing details of plot. In this way the writer lends suspense to the argument. This paragraph reveals the writer's thesis and is the climax of that suspense. It also brings in an "expert" to resolve the conflict. Since the writer's conclusions are clearly conjectural, she uses qualifying words like "may," "if," "suggests," and "implies."

As the story draws to a close Shirley Jackson seems to offer her own opinion about how the conflict will be resolved. The two people leading the attack on Mrs. Hutchinson are Mr. Adams and Mrs. Graves (p. 225). The name "Adams" suggests the first sinner, Adam. The rural setting and the opening paragraph suggest an idyllic place like the Garden of Eden. The name "Graves" alludes to a result of Adam's sin, Cain's murder of Abel. If Shirley Jackson intended these connections, the lottery may be symbolic of Original Sin, which, according to Christian dogma, is ineradicable and universal. All people—women, men, children, the youngest and the oldest, even

Christians (Mrs. Delacroix's name means "of the cross")—are tainted by Adam's fall. Thus, the villagers may give up lotteries in the form they now take, but Jackson implies that "lotteries" will always exist in some form or other and that human beings will always do evil just as eagerly as they do in this story.

NOTES

The footnote gives complete information about the primary source. It follows the form indicated in the *MLA Handbook*. It explains how the writer will handle subsequent references.

[1]"The Lottery," in Structure, Sound, and Sense, ed. Laurence Perrine, 2nd ed. (New York: Harcourt Brace Jovanovich, 1974), p. 219. All references to "The Lottery" will be to this edition and will appear in parentheses in the text.

SETTING IN NATHANIEL HAWTHORNE'S
"YOUNG GOODMAN BROWN"

The forest in Hawthorne's story "Young Goodman Brown" seems to represent sin. At least, the farther Goodman Brown journeys into the forest, the more he learns about the nature of sin and the more he suspects its presence in his village. But the forest also represents something else: Brown's psychological state during each stage of his journey.

Thesis. The implicit question answered by this thesis is, What does the forest represent?

When Brown takes his guilty leave of Faith ("What a wretch am I, to leave her on such an errand!"),[1] the forest has three main characteristics. First, it is dark; the road Brown has taken is "dreary" and "darkened by all the gloomiest trees of the forest" (p. 75). Second, it is hard to penetrate; the path is "narrow" and nearly obstructed by trees (p. 75). Finally, it causes fear; Brown feels that something threatening "may be concealed by the innumerable trunks and the thick boughs overhead"—perhaps an Indian or "the devil himself" (p. 75). The forest here represents Brown's recognition that he is entering the domain of evil (darkness is a traditional symbol of evil), that he cannot predict what will happen (he cannot see what lies ahead on the path), and that the consequences of his journey may be destructive (he is afraid).

Transition sentence. It announces the first stage of Brown's journey.

Topic sentence. It announces what the forest represents during the first stage of Brown's journey.

Once Brown has entered the forest, the devil joins him and initiates him into the knowledge of evil. One by one, the devil implicates individuals whom Brown particularly reveres: his grandfather, his father, Goody Cloyse, the minister, and Deacon Gookin. During this part of the story, Brown is confused about what really is true. The forest

Transition sentence. It announces the next stage of Brown's journey.

Topic sentence. It states

represents this confusion by its obscurity. It is
sunset when Brown enters the forest, but when
the devil appears, it has become "deep dusk" (p.
76), and when Goody Cloyse appears it is
"nightfall" (p. 78). Because of this increasing
darkness, Brown cannot be quite sure of what
he sees or hears. The devil's walking stick, for
example, seems to turn into a snake, but this
may be "an ocular deception, assisted by the
uncertain light" (p. 76). Brown thinks he hears
the voices of Deacon Gookin and the minister,
but "owing doubtless to the depth of the gloom
of that particular spot, neither the travellers
nor their steeds were visible" (p. 81). And he
seems to hear "a confused and doubtful sound
of voices," among whom are those of his fellow
townspeople, "both pious and ungodly" (p. 83),
when the next minute "he doubted whether he
had heard aught but the murmur of the old
forest, whispering without a wind" (p. 83).

Transition and topic
sentence.

Throughout the essay,
the organization of the
writer's evidence is
spatial. Plot details are
given in the order in
which they occur in the
story, and thus the essay
has a measure of
suspense. It builds
toward a climax. All of
the evidence, however,
directly relates to the
writer's thesis. The essay
does not merely give a
plot summary for its own
sake.

After the deacon and the minister leave,
the forest represents Brown's next
psychological state—disbelief. The part of the
forest into which the deacon and the minister
travel is "the heathen wilderness" where "no
church had ever been gathered or solitary
Christian prayed" (p. 82). Brown is on the
verge of taking this road—"he looked up to the
sky, doubting whether there really was a
heaven above him" (p. 82)—but resolves to go
no farther. Suddenly he suspects that Faith
herself, the person he most reveres, may be
engulfed by this forest of evil. He fancies that
he hears her voice, and he finds a pink ribbon
that might be hers. On this faint evidence, he
commits himself irrevocably to the forest: "My
Faith is gone," he cries, and rushes headlong
into the interior (p. 82).

Topic sentence.

Because of his disbelief Brown now enters

into a state of despair and insanity that the
forest mirrors perfectly:

A long quotation,
introduced by a colon,
indented and single-
spaced.

> The road grew wilder and drearier and
> more faintly traced, and vanished at
> length, leaving him in the heart of the
> dark wilderness, still rushing onward
> with the instinct that guides mortal man
> to evil. The whole forest was peopled with
> frightful sounds—the creaking of the
> trees, the howling of wild beasts, and the
> yell of Indians; while sometimes the wind
> tolled like a distant church bell, and
> sometimes gave a broad roar around the
> traveller, as if all Nature were laughing
> him to scorn. But he was himself the
> chief horror of the scene, and shrank not
> from its other horrors. (p. 84)

As he runs, Brown becomes a "demoniac" who
brandishes his staff with "frenzied gestures" (p.
84). His cries are in "unison" with the cry of
the forest (p. 85). It echoes his "horrid
blasphemy" and is a "tempest" that drives him
onward (p. 84).

Transition and topic
sentence. The climax of
the essay coincides with
the climax of the story.

At the climax of his frenzy, Brown sees
the next and final step in his journey—
complete alienation. Before him is a weird
scene that represents the rejection of all belief
in the goodness of human beings: a pulpitlike
rock surrounded by four pine trees whose tops
are on fire. Surrounding the pulpit is a
"congregation" of all the inhabitants, past and
present, of his village. The devil emerges to
complete Brown's initiation. The devil has
Faith brought in, and he asks the couple to
accept the existence of evil in everyone's soul:
"Evil is the nature of mankind. Evil must be
your only happiness. Welcome, again, my
children, to the communion of your race" (p.

88). But Brown balks at this final step. He tells Faith to "look up to Heaven, and resist the Wicked One" (p. 89). Immediately the forest changes. His frenzy has disappeared and so has the wild blaze of the forest.

Transition sentence. It relates to the experience described in the preceding paragraph and also to the whole experience of Brown's journey.

Topic sentence. It summarizes the total effect of the journey on Brown's mental state.

Hawthorne leaves us with a question of whether Brown's experience was a dream: "Had Goodman Brown fallen asleep in the forest and only dreamed a wild dream of a witch-meeting?" (p. 90). But the question is probably irrelevant, since the effect on Brown is the same as if his experience had really happened. Brown is a changed man. He has, it seems, in fact taken the final step urged upon him by the devil. He sees all people as hypocrites who pretend to be good but secretly worship and follow the devil. He even shrinks "from the bosom of Faith," scowling and muttering when he sees her at prayer. He has become a cold man, just as the forest when he awakens is "chill and damp" and "besprinkled . . . with the coldest dew" (p. 89).

The writer makes one final point about Brown's mental state and the forest, saying that even here, in the last stage of the journey, the forest represents Brown's attitude.

NOTES

[1]The Portable Hawthorne, ed. Malcolm Cowley (New York: Viking Press, 1948), p. 75. All references to "Young Goodman Brown" are to this edition and will appear in parentheses in the text.

POINT OF VIEW IN
EDWIN ARLINGTON ROBINSON'S
"RICHARD CORY"

Yvor Winters, a leading American critic, condemns Edwin Arlington Robinson's poem "Richard Cory" for containing "a superficially neat portrait of the elegant man of mystery" and for having a "very cheap surprise ending."[1] It is true that because Richard Cory fits the stereotype of "the man who has everything," his suicide at the end is surprising, even shocking. But the poet's handling of point of view makes the portrait of Richard Cory only apparently superficial and the ending only apparently "cheap."

In the second line of the poem, we learn that the speaker is not Robinson himself (the omniscient narrator), but someone with a limited view of things. He is one of the "people" of the town.[2] It is as if he has cornered a visitor on a sidewalk somewhere and is telling him about a fellow townsman whose suicide has puzzled and troubled him. He cannot understand it, so he talks about it. Throughout this speaker's narration, we learn a lot about him and his peers and how they regarded Richard Cory.

Clearly they saw him as something special. The imagery of kings and nobility ("crown," "imperially slim" and "richer than a king") permeates their conception of Richard Cory. To them he had the bearing and trappings of royalty. He was a "gentleman," a word that suggests courtliness as well as nobility. He had good taste ("he was always quietly arrayed"). He was wealthy. He had good breeding (he was "admirably schooled in every grace"). He "glittered when he walked," suggesting, perhaps, that he wore jewelry and walked with confidence. Because of this attitude, the speaker and his peers placed themselves in an almost feudal relationship to Cory. They saw themselves as "people on the pavement," as if they walked on the ground and Richard Cory somehow walked above them. Even if he did not literally walk above them, they saw him as "above" them socially. They seemed to think it unusual that he was "human when he talked." The word "human" suggests several things. One is that the people saw Cory as somehow exempt from the problems and restrictions of being a human being (thus "human") but that when he talked, he stepped out of character. Another is that he, who was so much above them, could be kind, warm, and thoughtful (another meaning of "human"). They were so astonished by this latter quality that when he did such a simple and obvious thing as say "Good-morning," he "fluttered pulses."

> The writer interprets a key word to support the essay's argument. Such interpretations are often necessary in analyzing poetry, since the weight of a poem's meaning often rests on the nuances of words.

In the final stanza, the speaker brings out the most important differences between the people and Richard Cory. Most obvious is that he was rich and they were poor; they "went without the meat, and cursed the bread." But another difference is suggested by the word "light": "So on we worked, and waited for the light." "Light" in this context most apparently means a time when things will be better, as in the expression "the light at the end of the tunnel." But another meaning of "light" is revelation. Light has traditionally symbolized knowledge and truth, and it may be that this is the meaning the speaker—or at least Robinson—has in mind. If so, another difference that the people saw between Richard Cory and themselves was that Cory had knowledge and understanding and they did not.

> Transition and topic sentence.

> Interpretation of a key word.

After all, they had no time to pursue knowledge; they needed all their time just to survive. But Richard Cory did have the time. He was a man of leisure who had been "schooled." If anyone would have had the "light"—a right understanding of things—then Richard Cory would have been that person.

Transition and topic sentence

Although Robinson does not tell us why Richard Cory killed himself, he leaves several hints. One of these is the assumptions about Richard Cory held by the narrator and the "people." Cory may have been a victim of their attitude. The poem gives no evidence that he sought to be treated like a king or that he had pretensions to nobility. He seems, in fact, to have been democratic enough. Although rich, well-mannered, and tastefully dressed, he nonetheless came to town, spoke with kindness to the people, and greeted them as if they deserved his respect. Could he even have wanted their friendship? But the people's attitude may have isolated Richard Cory. Every time he came to town, they stared at him as if

The line reference is necessary here because there is no easy-to-find quotation, but rather a reference to an event in the poem. Without the line reference, readers might find it difficult to spot the specific place in the poem that the writer has in mind.

he were a freak in a sideshow (ll. 1–2). In their imagination, furthermore, they created an ideal of him that was probably false and, if taken seriously by Richard Cory, would have been very difficult to live up to. Cory did not, at least, have the "light" that the people thought he had. His suicide attests to that. He was, in short, as "human" as they; but, unlike them, he lacked the consolation of fellowship. Ironically, then, the people's very admiration of Richard Cory, which set him apart as more than human and isolated him from human companionship, may have been the cause of his death.

The writer concludes by returning to the central issue raised at the beginning of the essay, bringing the critic's

Had Robinson told Cory's story as an omniscient narrator, Winters' complaint about the poem would be justified. The poem would seem to be an attempt to shock us with a

interpretation back into
the essay.

melodramatic and too-obvious irony. But Robinson has deepened the poem's meaning by having one of Cory's fellow townspeople tell his story. This presentation of Cory's character, his relationship to the townspeople, and his motives for suicide opens the poem up to interpretation in a way that Winters does not acknowledge or explore.

NOTES

[1]Yvor Winters, Edwin Arlington Robinson (Norfolk, Conn.: New Directions, 1946), p. 52.

[2]Tilbury Town: Selected Poems of Edwin Arlington Robinson (New York: Macmillan, 1951), p. 38. Further references to "Richard Cory" are to this edition and will appear in parentheses in the text.

TONE IN EMILY DICKINSON'S
"BECAUSE I COULD NOT STOP FOR DEATH"

Like the "Richard Cory" essay, this essay uses someone else's ideas as a starting point.

Thesis.

One of the questions raised in class about Emily Dickinson's "Because I Could Not Stop for Death" was whether or not its tone is optimistic. My feeling is that it is partly pessimistic and that Dickinson communicates that pessimism in the poem's imagery, its structure, its diction, and, in one crucial place, its rhythm.

The writer keeps the opposite position in view and represents it fairly and fully.

The tone of the first half of the poem (the first three stanzas) seems optimistic. As was suggested in class, the speaker seems to feel a special and warm relationship to Death, perhaps even to the point of seeing Death as a groom. He comes in a carriage, "kindly" stops for her, rides with only her inside, and takes his time. She in turn seems to be putting away the things of childhood (her "labor" and "leisure") in response to his "Civility."[1] She makes a symbolic journey through life with him, just as she would with a husband. Her carriage passes children at school (youth), "Fields of Gazing Grain" (maturity), and the "Setting Sun" (old age) (ll. 9–12). Her light, probably white, clothing (a gossamer gown and tulle scarf, mentioned in ll. 15–16) further suggests the marriage relationship. Altogether, in the first three stanzas, the narrator seems to feel cozy in her relationship with Death. She feels that Death is a friendly and kind companion. She is optimistic about where Death is taking her.

This poem is a little longer than "Richard Cory." Line numbers, even for quotations, may thus be helpful.

The tone shifts, however, with the first line of the fourth stanza (the beginning of the second half of the poem): "Or rather—he passed Us—" (l. 13). Several signals suggest this shift. One is the narrator's loss of momentum. She is now acted upon. The sun passes her. Since the sun traditionally represents life and the sunset death, I take this to mean that she has now died. Another signal is the change in rhythm. Up to this point, the rhythm has been a very regular iambic beat, almost a singsong. But the first line in the fourth stanza completely distorts that pattern, almost as if the regular beating of the heart has been jerkily disrupted. In the last part of the line, Dickinson substitutes one spondee (a foot with two accented syllables) for the two iambic feet that one would expect to be there. The result is that the last three words, which she isolates with dashes, all have about the same stress: "Ŏr ráthe̅r—Hé pássed Ús—." For me, the effect is as if something has come suddenly to a halt.

Transition and topic sentence.

It seems logical to associate this halt with the narrator's death, but I associate it also with her change of tone. Immediately after this line, she feels chilly. The sun has gone down (she is dead) and her clothes, which formerly were appropriate as wedding clothes, seem no longer adequate to warm her. Her gown is "only" gossamer, her tippet "only" tulle (11. 15–16). The chill of death is further underscored by her current place of residence, her grave:

> We passed before a House that seemed
> A Swelling of the Ground—. (11. 17–18)

Transition sentence.

In the final stanza, the narrator tells us that although "Centuries" have passed, it

> Feels shorter than the Day
> I first surmised the Horses Heads
> Were toward Eternity—. (11. 22–24)

The writer continues to represent the opposition.

Several people in class concluded that the tone of this final stanza is optimistic because the

narrator is in "Eternity" and that time in an
earthly sense passes very quickly for her. But
this stanza may well have an ironic twist that
suggests a pessimistic tone. At the end of the
first stanza she says that the carriage held
herself, Death, and "Immortality." But in the
last stanza she says that she "surmises" the
horses were headed "toward Eternity." It seems
possible that the narrator sees a difference
between the concepts "Immortality" and
"Eternity." The Oxford English Dictionary[2]
defines "immortal" as meaning "deathless,"
"undying," "living forever," and as "pertaining
to immortal beings or immortality." Almost all
the historical quotations that follow these
definitions in the OED associate "immortal"
with life after death, particularly life in
"heaven." The word "eternal," however, does
not necessarily include this idea. Eternity is
simply "infinite in past and future duration;
without beginning or end." Eternity can exist
even though one is dead. The word can also
express weariness or disgust over something
"that seems to be going on for ever." Thus
"immortality" is a more optimistic concept
than "eternity." Another nuance of the last
stanza is provided by the word "surmised." The
OED says that "surmise" means "to form a
notion that the thing in question may be so, on
slight grounds or without proof; to infer
conjecturally." Thus the narrator does not
know for certain where she is; she could (and
can) only guess. The final stanza may be
saying, then, that after her death, the narrator
guessed ("surmised") that Death was taking
her not to Immortality but only to Eternity. So
traumatic was this discovery that although
centuries have passed since then, they have not
seemed as long as that day seemed.

Topic sentence.

Interpretation of key
words in the poem.

Use of a reference work
to bolster the argument.

Interpretation of another
key word.

A summary of the
writer's interpretation of
the final stanza—put,
appropriately, at the end
of the paragraph.

The writer concludes by looking at the whole poem in light of the points established in the essay. The writer not only restates the thesis but offers an interpretation of the whole poem based on that thesis.

By the end of the poem, we have learned from the narrator's tone that she is left in a bad way. Whereas before her death she thought that Death was kind, she is now cold and without adequate clothing. She is alone. And she is filled with doubt and uncertainty. She may in time gain "immortality," but it is also possible that she has only gained the bleak, cold wasteland of "Eternity."

NOTES

[1]The Poems of Emily Dickinson, ed. Thomas H. Johnson (Cambridge, Mass.: Harvard University Press, 1955), II, 546, 11. 7–8. Further references to "Because I Could Not Stop for Death" are to this edition and will appear in parentheses in the text.

[2]The Oxford English Dictionary, ed. James A. H. Murray et al., 13 vols. (Oxford: Oxford University Press, 1933).

OEDIPUS' RESPONSIBILITY IN SOPHOCLES'
OEDIPUS REX

The writer identifies a problem of interpretation in the play.

       One of the most puzzling aspects of Sophocles' play Oedipus Rex is that Oedipus at the end accepts full responsibility for what he has done. After horribly maiming himself by gouging out his eyes, he proclaims to the Choragos:

>   This punishment
> That I have laid upon myself is just.
> If I had eyes,
> I do not know how I could bear the sight
> Of my father, when I came to the house of
>   Death,
> Or my mother: for I have sinned against
>   them both
> So vilely that I could not make my peace
> By strangling my own life.[1]

The writer summarizes the meaning of the quote in his own words.

The writer raises a specific question about the play.

Thesis. The thesis is the writer's answer to the question.

       In other words, he declares himself a "sinner" and accepts full responsibility for what he has done by inflicting the worst punishment upon himself that he can imagine, even worse than death. Yet throughout the play it seems as if Oedipus was fated to do these things and actually did them in spite of his efforts to avoid doing them. How, then, can Oedipus justifiably accuse himself of wrongdoing? Why doesn't he simply excuse himself by saying that he had done his best but fate was against him, that he had no control over what happened and therefore cannot be blamed? The answer to this question, I believe, is that although Oedipus may have been fated to do these actions, he nonetheless does them on purpose. It may even be that the oracle's pronouncements are more like forecasts or conjectures than prophecies. Knowing something about Oedipus' temperament would enable us to predict at least some of the things he did.

Transition and topic sentence.

We learn a lot about Oedipus' temperament in the first part of the play. In the opening scenes he appears as a proud and intemperate man. He enters treating his subjects as inferiors (he calls them "children") whom he, who bears the "famous name," will save (Prologue, l. 8). He anticipates the moment when he can play the hero, just as he did when he solved the riddle of the Sphinx. To this end, he has sent Creon to the Delphic Oracle to learn "what act or pledge of mine may save the city" (Prologue, l. 74). When Creon returns to say that the murderer of the previous king, Laios, must be found, Oedipus places an extremely harsh edict against the murderer; he must be "driven from every house," not spoken to, and his life "consumed in evil and wretchedness" (Scene I, ll. 20–31). Teiresias, the blind seer, calls attention to Oedipus' intemperate nature (Scene I, l. 109), and Oedipus suddenly and irrationally accuses Teiresias of planning Laios' murder:

The method of documentation for plays is to identify act, scene, and line numbers, when the play has them. Otherwise, give page numbers.

> You planned it, you had it done, you all but
> Killed him with your own hands.   (Scene I, ll. 128–129)

He rails at Teiresias—"You sightless, witless, senseless, mad old man!" (Scene I, l. 153)— and boasts that he is a better exorcist than Teiresias. Oedipus compounds his rash behavior by accusing Creon of the murder as well. Creon quite reasonably requests that Oedipus should at least present evidence against him, but Oedipus ignores him and says, "It is your death I want" (Scene II, l. 106). Throughout the first part of the play, in short,

The writer summarizes the meaning of the

Oedipus overreacts passionately, even violently, to events, especially when they challenge his pride or authority.

It is possible to see Oedipus overreacting in the same passionate and violent way when he kills his father. When he tells Iocasta why he left Corinth, there is at least a hint that he had been coddled, perhaps spoiled as a child. He was adopted (he learns later in the play) by the king and queen, a childless couple who did everything in their power to protect him from the truth about his origins. And he says that he "grew up chief among the men of Corinth" (Scene II, 1. 248). After he left Corinth (to escape the oracle's prediction), he came upon King Laios traveling with five attendants. The groom forced Oedipus off the road at Laios' command. At this point Oedipus became very angry and in his "rage" struck the groom back. Laios then hit Oedipus with his "double goad." With his club, Oedipus knocked Laios out of the chariot and onto the ground (Scene II, 11. 275–287). Up to this point, Oedipus had acted as any spoiled, egocentric, and spirited person might act. He paid back in kind what he had received by way of insult. He might have behaved more humbly and temperately, but he at least gave back only slightly more than he had received. But what he did next was completely out of line with what had gone before. After saying that Laios "rolled on the ground," Oedipus says: "I killed him/I killed them all" (Scene II, 1. 288). Assuming that Laios had not been killed by the blow that knocked him from the chariot, what Oedipus did was terrible. First he attacked an old man lying defenseless on the ground and killed him. Then he attacked all the rest, killing all he could (one, a "household servant," escaped). Because of Oedipus' pride—his sense of personal injury—he inflicted punishment on writer not only summarizes the meaning of the evidence presented in the paragraph, but also ties the evidence to the main thesis of the essay.

Transition and topic sentence.

Transition and topic sentence.

these people far in excess of what they deserved. And although Oedipus did not premeditatedly kill his father, he did so without just cause. He is guilty of murder. And he is close to doing the same thing at the beginning of the play, when he demands the death penalty for the innocent Creon.

Oedipus' high-handed way of meting out punishment brings up another flaw in his character, his inability to take the gods seriously. One might argue that had Oedipus taken the gods seriously, he would have remained in Corinth and awaited his fate humbly and courageously. Instead, he takes matters into his own hands, as if he could by his own actions escape the decrees of heaven. This feeling of independence, even defiance of the gods, is illustrated even more clearly when he and Iocasta gloat over having apparently outmaneuvered the gods' predictions. "Ah!" Oedipus says,

> Why should a man respect the Pythian hearth, or
> Give heed to the birds that jangle above his head?
> They prophesied that I should kill Polybos,
> Kill my own father; but he is dead and buried,
> And I am here—I never touched him, never,
> Unless he died of grief for my departure,
> And thus, in a sense, through me. No. Polybos
> Has packed the oracles off with him underground.
> They are empty words. (Scene III, ll. 917–926)

The most important result of Oedipus' refusal to take the gods seriously is his

The writer states an alternative interpretation and then argues against it. In other words, he anticipates the readers' potential objections and questions.

marriage to Iocasta. It is true that Oedipus would understandably have had his guard down when he came to Thebes. He thought he was far from the land where his father and mother lived. He came as a hero, the savior of the city, and was invited to be king. To seal his status as king, he married the former queen. But, after all, Iocasta was old enough to be his mother— obviously. Even if he still thought that Merope was his mother, he might have considered the spirit of the oracle's pronouncement, not just the letter. It is possible to sleep with one who is <u>like</u> one's mother, even if that person is not literally so. In such a case, the sin of incest is no less a reality. Iocasta seems to recognize this possibility when she says, "How many men, in dreams, have lain with their mothers!" (Scene III, 1. 68). Oedipus' relationship with Iocasta, furthermore, is warm and close. It is more than just a state marriage entered into merely to secure power. And it is clearly sexual, since he has produced at least four children over a long period of time. The result, then, may be that Oedipus has committed incest in his mind long before it becomes a public, legal fact. The fact that Iocasta is his real mother can be seen as purely an accident. The existence of his incest would have been equally real without it.

The conclusion summarizes the points made in the essay and reemphasizes the validity of the thesis.

What I have tried to show in this essay is that although on the surface Oedipus seems a victim of fate, actually he participates in that fate enough to be responsible for it. He is impetuous, proud, violent, unjust, and heedless of the gods. As such, he is to blame for killing his father and committing incest with his mother. He finally and justly recognizes his blame, accepts responsibility for it, and punishes himself.

NOTES

The "Exodos" is the concluding section of the play.

[1]Oedipus Rex, trans. Dudley Fitts and Robert Fitzgerald (New York: Harcourt Brace Jovanovich, 1949), Exodos, 11. 140—147. References to Oedipus Rex are to this edition and appear in parentheses in the text.

CÉLIMÈNE'S COQUETRY IN MOLIÈRE'S
THE MISANTHROPE

Célimène's coquetry is one of the mainsprings of action in Molière's play The Misanthrope. But why is she a coquette? Does she keep men on a string with her "most melting and receptive manner"[1] only to flatter her vanity? Is she merely the "beautiful woman without kindness"? My view of Célimène is much more sympathetic than this. I see her as a potential victim who must defend herself against a predatory world with the only weapon at her disposal, her coquetry.

That Célimène's world is predatory and that she is vulnerable seem clear by the time the play is over. In the first place, her world is one of constant struggle. Both she and Alceste are involved in lawsuits before the play begins, and Alceste becomes involved in a second (with Oronte) almost immediately. The causes of the first two lawsuits remain unidentified, but if they are anything like the cause of the lawsuit with Oronte, they are trivial. It seems as if one could end up at law over almost anything, even over words spoken in unguarded moments. The struggle in Célimène's society, however, is more than just legal. People are constantly gossiping with the sole intention of doing others harm. Of all the gossips, the most malicious is Arsinoé, who actually comes to Célimène's house to engage in a pitched battle of insult trading. Célimène herself is daily confronted with a struggle over her person and, presumably, her fortune. Her coquetry may exacerbate this struggle, but the struggle would still exist without it. Her suitors vie with one another for first place in her attentions and bombard her with jealousy and possessiveness.

The writer raises specific questions about the play.

Thesis. The thesis is the writer's answer to these questions.

Transition and topic sentence. Note the logic of the writer's organization. Before the essay can show that Célimène uses coquetry to defend herself, it must first show that something threatens her.

Transition and topic sentence. The essay moves to the next logical step in the organization. It must now show that Célimène has no means of protecting herself other than her coquetry. This paragraph eliminates one traditional means of protection: family.

Célimène's main need is for a protector. Normally, a family would shield a young woman from those who would do her harm, particularly suitors who might turn out to be disastrous husbands. But Célimène has no family to speak of. Her cousin Éliante is the only relative we see, and although Éliante is "honest," she has no power to help Célimène. No one in her society, furthermore, is a fitting substitute for her parents, a fact that Célimène seems to recognize. Her gossip session in Act II with Acaste and Clitandre may not show her in the best light, but it at least shows that she is clearsighted about her social peers. She describes them as blunderers, bores, social climbers, egomaniacs, paranoid fantasizers, and pretentious fools. She sees that hypocrisy dominates her society, and we see from Alceste's portrait of the man suing him that such hypocrisy can be dangerous:

> Call him knave, liar, scoundrel, and all the
>   rest,
> Each head will nod, and no one will
>   protest.   (I, 11. 135–136)

Transition and topic sentence. This paragraph eliminates a second means of protection: marriage. Note that even though it is a separate paragraph, it nonetheless continues to develop the major topic introduced in the above paragraph: Célimène's need for a protector.

Célimène could provide herself with a protector by getting married. But her suitors are all a sorry lot. Acaste, Clitandre, and Oronte are vain and foppish. Her portraits of each in the letters revealed in Act V accurately reflect what we see of them in the rest of the play. This leaves Alceste. Alceste has good grounds for criticizing his society, and it may be that because he does so he is more admirable than his passive and fatalistic friend, Philinte. Also, it may be that Célimène "loves" Alceste. At the end he is the only suitor to whom she feels a need to confess:

> I've wronged you, I confess it; and in
>   my shame
> I'll make no effort to escape the blame.
> The anger of those others I could despise;
> My guilt toward you I sadly
>   recognize.   (V, 11. 304–307)

She even offers to let him marry her (V, 1.
347).

Topic sentence.

But Alceste would not be likely to give
Célimène the protection she needs, a fact that
she seems to sense. He has many flaws. One
flaw is a lack of moderation. He takes extreme
positions on everything. In the face of human
error, he claims that "all are corrupt" (I, 1.
89). Rather than flatter others, he would hang
himself (I, 1. 28). Rather than work out his
differences with society, he would remove to a
"wild, trackless place" where he could "forget
the human race" (V, 11. 327–329). Rather
than help Célimène, he would force her to
choose between him and other human society;
he would punish her with total separation
from other people. A second flaw is
inconsistency. Even though Alceste states his
opinions in the strongest possible language, he
cannot act upon them. He claims to love
honesty, consistency, and plain dealing, yet he
ignores Éliante, who loves him and who fits his
ideal, and instead he pursues Célimène, who
feigns indifference and seems the opposite of
his ideal. He threatens to withdraw his
attentions from Célimène, but cannot do
so when the crisis comes. Even in trivial
things he is inconsistent. In Act II (Scenes
IV and V) he says that he will go, but he
stays.

Topic sentence. Although
this paragraph develops

A third flaw is Alceste's lack of sound
judgment. His attack on Oronte's poetry in Act

the topic introduced in the preceding paragraph, the writer begins a new paragraph at a logical break in the line of thought in order to provide a visual rest for readers. Otherwise the paragraph would be uncomfortably long.

I, for example, seems groundless. He produces little evidence to support his opinions, and the poetry that he offers as a model of good poetry seems little different from Oronte's. His accusation in Act IV that Célimène has betrayed him is based on an unsigned, unaddressed letter that could have been written by someone else and not necessarily to a man. He even believes the person who gives him the letter, Arsinoé, although he knows her to be Célimène's bitterest rival. Overall, his jealousy of Célimène is a self-fulfilling prophecy. He is jealous before there is evidence of betrayal and thus helps to bring about that betrayal. A fourth flaw is his willful and irrational contradictoriness. Célimène says,

> He lives in deadly terror of agreeing,
> 'Twould make him seem an ordinary
>   being.
> Indeed, he's so in love with contradiction,
> He'll turn against his most profound
>   conviction
> And with a furious eloquence deplore it,
> If only someone else is speaking for
>   it.   (II, ll. 229–234)

Molière verifies the accuracy of this observation by having Philinte, the most moderate and reasonable man in the play, agree with it. A fifth flaw is Alceste's failure to truly love Célimène as a woman would want to be loved. The love he offers only adds to the strife that threatens her. She tells him:

> If all hearts beat according to your
>   measure,
> The dawn of love would be the end of
>   pleasure;

And love would find its perfect
  consummation
In ecstasies of rage and reprobation. (II,
  11. 261–264)

Rather, Éliante adds, men should "love their
ladies even for their flaws" (II, 1. 284).

Topic sentence.
The flaw that most seriously undermines
Alceste's ability to protect Célimène is his lack
of practicality. If she is to have a protector, she
needs someone who can win—or avoid—the
battles that inevitably occur in this society. Yet
Alceste seems to enjoy alienating everyone in
sight, even his good friends. Such behavior will
make him a magnet for every contentious
crackpot who has the time, money, and power
to battle and possibly destroy him. Even worse,
he does not care about winning these battles.
He would willfully and quixotically lose them
just to make a point. He refuses, for example, to
contest the unfavorable verdict of his lawsuit,
no matter what "cruel penalty it may bring"
(V, 1. 61), just so it can serve

As a great proof and signal demonstration
Of the black wickedness of this
  generation. (V, 11. 65–66)

Transition and topic
sentence. Having shown
that Célimène has no
traditional means of
defense, the writer now
can argue that she must
defend herself with her
coquetry.
The corruption of her society and the
flaws of the one man she cares for leave
Célimène little choice about how to conduct
herself. She seems unable at this point in her
life to give up society:

What! I renounce the world at my age,
And die of boredom in some
  hermitage? (V, 11. 334–335)

She is, after all, very young—only twenty—and
not fully cognizant of what she wants. "Her

heart's a stranger to its own emotion," Éliante
says:

> Sometimes it thinks it loves, when no
>   love's there;
> At other times it loves quite
>   unaware. (IV, 11. 50–52)

She has no family and no reliable friends to
protect her. So her reaction, perhaps
instinctual, is to gain power by the only
weapon at her disposal, her coquetry. With this
power she protects herself from those who
would do her harm. She tells Alceste, for
example, that she keeps Clitandre in tow
because he can help her in her lawsuit (II, 11.
45–46), and she encourages Acaste because he
is a gossip who, though "no great help," could
do her "harm" (II, 11. 100–101). Her
encounter with Arsinoé is a tribute to her
power; Arsinoé comes to Célimène because
Célimène has the power to retain something
that both want, Alceste's devotion. And
Célimène's victory in this scene shows that she
has learned how to maintain her power with
other weapons approved by her society, her
tongue and her wit. Another tribute to
Célimène's power is paid by Alceste late in the
play:

Topic idea completed.

> Yes, I could wish that you were
>   wretchedly poor,
> Unloved, uncherished, utterly obscure;
> That fate had set you down upon the
>   earth
> Without possessions, rank, or gentle
>   birth;
> Then, by the offer of my heart, I might
> Repair the great injustice of your plight;

I'd raise you from the dust, and proudly
prove
The purity and vastness of my love.   (IV,
11. 294–301)

In effect, Alceste is admitting that because
Célimène's power is equal to his, he cannot
make her do what he wants. And although he
may regret this state of affairs, we can see that
Célimène's power gives her the option to
choose and that her coquetry is a means of
testing and thus weeding out undesirable
suitors. Were she as weak as Alceste wishes,
she would have no options. She would have to
marry the first protector who came along, no
matter how unsuitable.

Rather than conclude by summarizing the points of the argument, the writer assumes that the essay has made its point and instead speculates about what will happen to Célimène in the future. But in order to do this, the writer must restate the thesis and thus return readers to the questions raised at the beginning.

What will happen to Célimène in the
future? Will her life turn out well or badly? The
end of the play does not offer much hope for
her. Alceste seems the same as he was at the
beginning. And Célimène seems forced to follow
the same course that she has followed up to
now. Perhaps as she grows older she will
become more mature and will help to stabilize
the mercurial Alceste. But if Célimène cannot
find a protector, she will ultimately have to
discover some means of gaining power other
than coquetry, for the strength of her coquetry
comes from her beauty, and her beauty will
decline as she grows older. Arsinoé is a graphic
example of a woman who, because she has lost
her youthful beauty, must grasp at power
through hypocrisy, subterfuge, and slander. We
can only hope that the youthful, charming, and
beautiful Célimène will somehow avoid a
similar fate.

NOTES

[1]The Misanthrope, trans. Richard Wilbur (New York: Harcourt Brace Jovanovich, 1955), II, 1. 22. References to The Misanthrope are to this edition and will appear in parentheses in the text.

Index of Terms

Index of Authors and Works

A 1
B 2
C 3
D 4
E 5
F 6
G 7
H 8
I 9
J 0